JERUSALEM

Medieval map of the world, with Jerusalem at
its center.

JERUSALEM

PREFACE BY

ISAAC BEN-ZVI

PRESIDENT OF ISRAEL

EDITED BY

Dr. MICHAEL AVI-YONAH

PROFESSOR OF ARCHAEOLOGY

THE HEBREW UNIVERSITY

ART-EDITOR

S. J. SCHWEIG

ARCO PUBLISHING COMPANY, INC.

NEW YORK, N.Y.

Library of Congress Catalogue Card Number:
60-8358

Jerusalem, February 15, 1960.

Prof. Dr. M. Avi-Yonah, Editor
"The Holy City of Jerusalem"
The Israeli Publishing Institute,
Jerusalem.

Dear Professor Avi-Yonah,

Jerusalem is the Holy City not only to the nation of Israel, but to all three of the monotheistic religions. The holiness of the city comes to it from its glorious past. Jerusalem was the spiritual and religious cradle of civilization. But her importance is also derived from the fact that she was the center of the spiritual and political life of the people of Israel.

I am glad to take this opportunity to deliver sincere best wishes for this undertaking whose purpose is to set forth Jerusalem, the city—the chronicles of her past, her scenes and views, her sons and citizens, her streets and alleys, her newer sections and the suburbs that arise around her as she grows today.

This book sets before everyone, in Israel and out, the experience of Jerusalem—city of the past and mother of the nations—in her renewed glory of today, portrayed in the fullness and freshness of the colorful photography. It will be a highly valuable substitute for all those who cannot see it for themselves and a supplement for those who have had the privilege of seeing Jerusalem.

I have no doubt that the names of the editors themselves are indicative of the highly authorized level of its contents and photographs and that there is enough contained in this book to fulfill the task which it has undertaken for those who love the Holy City. It will make possible the recognition of Jerusalem as the capital of Israel and indeed of the world.

Isaac Ben-Zvi

President of the State of Israel

One hundred and fifty generations ago Jerusalem was a Canaanite town of no particular significance, then called Yarah-Shalem, meaning "Shalem the god founded it." The town stood on a small outcrop of rock, extending below what is today the southeastern part of the Old City, between the Kidron Valley and a smaller cleft to the west. For the first two thousand years of its existence it showed little development; then it became the capital of a succession of kings who ruled over the city itself and the small state around it.

Three thousand years ago David, the anointed king of a united Israel, conquered Jerusalem, and by this act set Jerusalem apart from all other cities. As we leaf through the pages of the Scriptures, the name and image of the Holy City appear on nearly every page. After David, the warrior and poet, came Solomon, the builder of the Temple. In the following centuries some of the greatest biblical figures, Isaiah, the noble son of Amoz, and Jeremiah, the humble peasant of Anatot, added vibrant chapters to the city's history. In the course of the ages the spirit which animates the Jewish nation developed and flourished here. Here the canon of the Bible was completed and its central ideas of faith, justice and ethics were elaborated. These still dominate mankind, through Judaism and through the creeds which flowed out from it, Christianity and Islam.

The story of the Holy City is one of an arduous and spirited endeavour to overcome the handicap of a geographical location which by no means favored the creation of a great city. Furthermore, the land was poor and there were few springs and little rain. It is, too, the story of constant contention against immensely powerful neighbors who held sway over the ancient Orient and sought to transform the spirit of the Holy City with their hosts of soldiers, governors and tax collectors, merchants and financiers. This struggle began with the great dynasts of the Nile and Euphrates Valleys and is being waged even in our own day.

Of all the great cities of antiquity Jerusalem is unique in being so often described in detail. The sanctuary of Solomon and the royal house set in its vicinity are described in detail in I Kings, 6-7 and II Chronicles 3-4. When, after the first return to Zion, the city was restored to some of its former glory, its governor, Nehemiah, left an account of its appearance at that time and what he did to repair the breaches in its walls (Neh. 2, 3 and 12). And again, in the last days of the Second Temple, Josephus Flavius prefaced his description of the great siege by Titus with a report on the condition of the city and its defenses in 70 A.D. His description of the Temple Mount complements the particulars given in those two tractates of the Mishna which deal with the "Measures" (Middot) of the edifice and the "Daily Sacrifice" (Tammid). More facts about the Jerusalem of the Second Temple can be gleaned from the vast Talmudic lore.

With the beginning of the Christian pilgrimages, and in particular with the recognition of Christianity as the official religion of the Roman Empire under Constantine, the pilgrims' texts provided a growing source of information. Starting with an anonymous traveller who went from Bordeaux in Gaul to Jerusalem in 333 A.D., a vast travel literature has accumulated in which the most important names are Theodosius and Antonius of Placentia in the sixth century, Arculfus in the eighth, Felix Fabri in the fifteenth and Quaresmius in the seventeenth century. Each of these travellers naturally devoted most of his space to the Holy City and holy places and edifices.

Modern scientific research into the topography and archeology of Jerusalem may be said to have begun with the arrival of the American scholar, E. Robinson, in 1838. The growing interest in an exact exploration of the remains of the ancient Holy City led to the establishment of the Palestine Exploration Fund, to the mapping of the city and its rock underground by the Ordnance Survey and to the first excavations (Tombs of the Kings by de Saulcy, the walls surrounding the Temple Mount by Warren). Since then excavations have hardly ceased in Jerusalem. Gradually the archeologists explored the Gihon tunnels, the Ophel and City of David and the First and Third Walls of the City. Today, only two major problems remain unsolved: the extent of the city in the time of the kings of Judah and the course of the Second Wall.

Since World War I and the establishment of the Mandate, scholars of the Jewish community in Jerusalem have taken an active part in its exploration. On behalf of the Jewish Palestine Exploration Society, Dr. Nahum Slouschz cleared the "Tomb of Absalom" and the late Professors Mayer and Sukenik the remains of the Third Wall. Since the establishment of the State of Israel this work has continued under the auspices of the Hebrew University and the Department of Antiquities: a Judean fortress of the eighth century B.C. was discovered at Ramat Rahel at the southern approaches to the city and in Alfasi Road, Rehavia Quarter, a Hasmonean tomb with drawings of a sea fight and the earliest known representations of the seven-branched candlestick of the Temple were found. The clearance of the mysterious tumuli west of the city by Ruth Amiran has not led to a complete clarification of their purpose, but further research will no doubt solve this riddle too.

While stressing the importance of the scientific interest in the remains of Jerusalem, we should always keep in mind that giving them life is the centuries-old involvement of the city with three of the world's great faiths.

In this Holy City, war was declared on the old pagan religions. Here the tender plant of the belief in one God took root, and was shaped into the message: "For out of Zion shall go forth the Law and the word of God from Jerusalem" (Isaiah 2:3). Wherever there is a Jewish community, it turns in prayer towards this sacred spot, morning, midday and evening.

Jerusalem is not holy to the Jews alone. In Jerusalem Christians follow in awe the stations of the Via Dolorosa which lead to the Church of Calvary and the Resurrection. Here stood the *Mater Ecclesiarum,* the church on Mount Zion which was the mother of all the other churches. Moslems the world over regard the Noble Sanctuary *(el-Haram esh-Sherif)* with the Dome of the Rock and the el-Aqsa Mosque as the third holiest place in the world.

The establishment of modern Jerusalem as the seat of the Government and Parliament of a resurrected Israel is in the eyes of Jews dispersed over the globe the inevitable fulfillment of the Divine promise as transmitted by the Prophets.

The Holy City, in both its mundane and spiritual aspects, is an expression of the ethical aspirations of mankind and of the everlasting rule of God's will as set out in the Scriptures.

THE PUBLISHERS

The approach of the New City from the west, which was paved after War of Liberation.

"As the mountains are round about
Jerusalem"—Psalms 125:2.
The Hills of Judah and Benjamin
around the city.

MEI NEFTOAH

ROMEMA

GIVAT SHAUL

E-TUR

NEVE SHA'ANAN

SILOAM

BAYIT VEGAN

QATAMON

MANAHAT

BEIT SAFAFA

JERUSALEM

In the hill country west of the Jordan River, the main highway follows the course of the watershed which twists down the Holy Land from North to south, separating the Mediterranean from the Dead Sea. Half way down it passes ancient Bethel—"the House of God," which has been a site of worship since earliest times—and mounts towards ancient Beetot, near modern Ramallah. Here it dips to the plateau of Gibeon—*el Jib,* another holy place, and then rises to a ridge called *Har Hazofim* in Hebrew, and in Greek, Mount Scopus, both meaning "The Mount of Beholding." For here pilgrims of untold generations have first looked upon the Holy City, Jerusalem, half hidden in a fold of ground formed by the Valley of the Son of Hinnom and the Kidron Valley. From Mount Scopus one sees another elevation, now crowned by the Monastery of Elias, and beyond, the mountains of Bethlehem and Hebron.

South of Mount Scopus the watershed swings westward across modern Jerusalem. Only in our own day, for the first time in history, has the city spread westward across the watershed. Ancient Jerusalem, even at the pinnacle of its glory, remained within the confines of the easterly Dead Sea region.

About half a mile southwest of Mount Scopus, approximately where today's highway reaches Jerusalem from the west, a secondary ridge leaves the watershed in a southeasterly direction. About half a mile down, branching off to the south, two subsidiary ridges enclose a valley: the valley of ancient Jerusalem. These two ridges help to form a system of three depressions shaped like a trident: the Valley of the Son of Hinnom on the west and south, the Valley of Jehoshaphat or Kidron on the east and the Central Valley. Within this area most of the history of Jerusalem has taken place.

Its juxtaposition to the watershed between the two seas has endowed Jerusalem with all the assets and burdened it with all the disadvantages of a city situated on the border between two different types of climatic, geological and geographical regions. Its precipitation and temperature are affected by both the Mediterranean and the desert regions. As a result, the flora of the Jerusalem area is between the Mediterranean and the Irano-Turanian steppe types, with the Saharo-Sindian desert region type only a short distance away. The geological division is almost identical. The Turanian area encompasses most of historic Jerusalem; the dry Senon in the east reaches almost down to the Kidron Valley; and the Cenomanian area, which encompasses modern Jerusalem, contains some of the best building stones in the country and was therefore of decisive importance in the building of the city.

Geography was of similar significance in determining the physical character of Jerusalem and, to a great extent, its history. Jerusalem is situated at some distance from the two main international thoroughfares crossing the Holy Land: the coastal road and the "king's highway" running east of the Jordan River from Eilat to Damascus. The remoteness from trade traffic, of course, made Jerusalem virtually a dead city commercially. Yet, it conferred upon the city advantages which more than compensated for the loss. In its aloofness from the major commercial and military arteries, Jerusalem was relatively untouched by the various streams of thought that swept through the Orient and, therefore, retained a relatively large degree of spiritual independence. Moreover, the difficulty of attacking the city saved it time and again from the vicissitudes which visited its apparently better situated neighbors. And if Jerusalem was unprofitably far from the international trade routes, it was, on the other hand, fairly well placed as regards internal communications. Its position near the watershed afforded it ready access to the principal north-south route of Canaan and, moreover, it was near the junction of this route and the east-west route coming from around the northern tip of the Dead Sea.

Today, the main arteries of communicaton of the New Jerusalem come from the west. Both road and rail gradually mount the Judean hills "that are round about Jerusalem" (Psalms 125:2) as they approach the city set high up on those hills. The observant traveller will note the contrast between the hills west of Jerusalem—once heavily wooded, then ravaged by time and history, and now being afforested once more—and the hills east of the city, whose barrenness bespeaks incipient desert. Here and there in those eastern hills some olive trees have survived, constituting a link between the old horticulture and the new.

Thy father was an Amorite and thy mother an Hittite

Ezekiel 16:2

THE CANAANITE CITY

The origins of Jerusalem are shrouded in the obscurity which engulfs the beginnings of many other famous places. It emerges into the light of history in what archeologists call the Early Bronze Age, which they place during the third millenium B.C. This period corresponds to that of the Old Kingdom of Egypt; as a matter of fact, it is in Egyptian sources that the name Jerusalem first appears. The Pharaohs of the 19th century B.C. would write the names of their vassals on little pottery figurines. Whenever a vassal proved unreliable, the figurine bearing his name was smashed and untold magical harm was done to him. These inscriptions, called "Execration Texts," have preserved, among other Canaanite names, the name *Urushamem,* which is Jerusalem. The two elements of the name are now understood to be "Yeru" and "Shalem," meaning "the god Shalem founded (the city)." Shalem is a well known deity of the ancient Western Semites, particularly the Amurru (Amorites). The saying of Ezekiel quoted at the head of this chapter is borne out by the connection of this god's name with the beginnings of Jerusalem.

From what we know of the general political and social history of the time, we can reconstruct, with what we believe to be reasonable certainty, the earliest aspects of Canaanite Jerusalem. Divided into numerous mounain and valley areas, Palestine does not naturally encourage the establishment of a unified state. Early Canaan, therefore, comprised many city-states. One of these was Jerusalem. The city limits seem to have included only its immediate vicinity, so that Gibeon and its cities to the north and Bethlehem and its cities to the south were independent of Jerusalem. Jerusalem could expand freely only to the east, towards the Desert.

Archeological research has established beyond doubt the location of Canaanite Jerusalem. In the whole area even of modern Jerusalem, there are only two natural springs: *Mei Nephtoah*—the Waters of Nephtoah near the western boundary of the city and the Spring of Gihon on the most eastern ridge mentioned in the Introduction.

The existence of the Spring of Gihon so close to a hill with such natural defensive strength—at least in the conditions of ancient warfare—led the Canaanites to select this hill as the site of their city. The natural declivities on three sides of the ridge fixed the line of the city's walls on the west, south and east. Three of the Canaanite city's gates—the Valley Gate on the west, the Fountain Gate on the south and the Water Gate on the East—were in use till Israelite times.

From its inception Jerusalem seems to have had strong religious associations. Already in the time of Abraham, the 18th century B.C., "Melchizedek King of Salem"—which is generally understood to refer to Jerusalem—was "Priest of the Most High God" and, as such, received from Abraham a tithe of the spoils he took from Chedarlaomer and his allies (Genesis 14:18-20). "Zedek," meaning "justice," was apparently part of the name of the priest-kings of the Canaanite-Jerusalem line; at any rate, we find Adoni-Zedek King of Jerusalem in the time of Joshua (Joshua 10:1, 26).

Jerusalem is again mentioned in Egyptian sources of the 15th and 14th centuries B.C., in the famous Tel el-Amarna letters, which are the diplomatic correspondence of the Pharaohs Amenhotep III and Amenhotep IV. (The latter is better known as Akhnaten or Ikhnaton, who unsuccessfully tried to institute monotheism in Egypt.) Occupying a prominent place in these letters is Abdihiba (or Puti-hiba) King of Jerusalem. Like most of his fellow rulers in the land, he time and again importuned the Egyptian monarch to help him against the "Habiru," a group of warlike tribes who are believed to be connected with the later Hebrews.

At the time of the Israelite conquest of Canaan, Jerusalem appears as a city of the Jebusites—a tribe of unknown origin believed to be connected with the Hittite nation, splinters of which penetrated Canaan in the 14th century B.C. Evidence that there was in Jerusalem at one time or other a Hittite element are the passage from Ezekiel quoted at the head of this chapter and the report of the residence there, in David's time, of Uriah the Hittite (I Samuel 11:3). In any case, we know from the account of Joshua's conquest that the King of Jerusalem was at the head of a coalition formed to punish the Gibeonites for defecting to the Israelites. The Canaanite

"The mountain of the Lord's house shall be established in the top of the mountains—"
Isaiah 2:2. View from the west.

The lower part of the Valley of Hinnom.

Inscription on a jug handle from the period of Nehemiah (444-432 B.C.) bearing the so-called "Seal of Solomon" and the letters YRSLM, or "Yerushalem," one of the ancient forms of the name of the city.

The Valley of Jehoshaphat or Kidron, where tradition, basing itself on Joel 3:2, 12, declares that the Final Judgment will take place. Shown here are, left: an ancient Jewish cemetery; center: the so-called "Pillar" or "Tomb of Absalom;" right background: Mount Moriah with a section of the wall of the Temple Mount at its summit.

General view of the Temple Mount
and the Old City from the slope of
the Mount of Olives to the east.

Early 19th century woodcut of Jaffa Gate.

24

Mount of Olives with Bethany in the right background. Bethany was the residence of Lazarus and his sisters Mary and Martha, and Jesus often went from Jerusalem to lodge there (Matthew 21:17, 26:6; Mark 11:1, 11-12; 14:3; Luke 19:29; 24:50; John 11:1, 18; 12:1). Tradition places the tomb of Lazarus here and the Arabs call the village el-Eizariyeh from el-Eizar, the Arabic form of Lazarus.

Egyptian clay figurine from the Middle Kingdom period, containing an "Execration Text" directed against the Pharaoh's enemies. The inscription shown here contains the first recorded mention of the name Jerusalem.

forces were defeated in the Valley of Ayalon, but Jerusalem did not share the fate of her allies and remained in Jebusite hands till the time of David. As a Jebusite city, Jerusalem constituted a barrier between the house of Joseph in the mountains of Ephraim and the tribe of Judah and its allies. When David set about uniting Israel, this foreign enclave became still more unbearable, especially as the Jebusites appear to have allied themselves against Israel with the Phillistines of the southern plain.

Nevertheless David took the stronghold of Zion: the same is the City of David

II Samuel 5:7

The storming of Jerusalem-Jebus was the first great accomplishment of the united Israelite nation after David was anointed king in Hebron in about 1003 B.C. The details of this great feat of arms are obscure and it appears to be connected with the mysterious *tsinnor*. Some scholars understand this word to mean a "water conduit" through which Joab and his men stole into the city. Others understand it to refer to some weapon with which the Israelites smote the Jebusites. Be that as it may, the fact of the conquest is undisputed and one of the most decisive events in the history of Jerusalem.

By taking the city, David united the territory of Israel; and by establishing his capital in this place which, although assigned to the tribe of Benjamin, had so far remained outside the tribal area, he avoided the inter-tribal jealousy which would have resulted from any other choice. At the same time, he raised Jerusalem from the status of merely another Canaanite

The well shown here was, with the Spring of Gihon, one of the only two water sources of ancient Jerusalem. It is known to the local populace as Bir Eyub (the Well of Job). Scholars identify it with the Biblical En Rogel (Joshua 15:7, 18:6; II Samuel 17:17; I Kings 1:9) and En Tanin (Dragon's Well—Nehemiah 2:13).

city-state to that of the chief city of a great nation. Soon, after extending his dominion over an area reaching from Nahal Mizraim—The Brook of Egypt (today known as *Wadi el-Arish*) to the Red Sea and the Euphrates River, he brought over the Ark of the Covenant—the national palladium—from Kiryat Ye'arim to Jerusalem (II Samuel 6). In so doing, he established Jerusalem also as the nation's religious center, although he was not granted the privilege of erecting a permanent Temple.

Soon after taking Jerusalem, David beat back two attempts by the Phillistines to re-establish their connection with the city. He seems to have spared the conquered inhabitants, however. Indeed, David used their administrative experience in organizing his court and executive bodies. He fortified the city anew, erecting in it a fortress called "Zion" (probably on the vulnerable north side of the city) and a "House of Mighty Men" on the south side. Exercising a privilege usually reserved for royalty, he had a dynastic tomb constructed inside the city: it was generally forbidden to bury the dead within Jerusalem's walls. Archeologists believe that they have located and excavated the site of the tomb and the stairs leading up to "The City of David" mentioned in Nehemiah 3:15 and 12:37.

Excavation shaft and tunnels used by the Palestine Exploration Fund at the wall of the Temple Mount in 1867-69.

And the King made silver to be in Jerusalem as stones

I Kings 10:27

THE REIGN OF SOLOMON

In contrast with David's martial reign, that of his son Solomon (970-930 B.C.) was devoted largely to economic expansion and building activities. In the last years of Solomon's reign, Damascus successfully revolted, reducing the area controlled from Jerusalem. Before that, however, Solomon exploited to the utmost the city's advantageous position on the trade routes joining the Mediterranean and the Red Sea. His trading activities—which included the exportation of copper from the Aravah in the south, the importation of gold from Ophir and serving as middleman in the horse trade between Asia Minor and Egypt—flourished, thus enabling him to indulge in the royal pastime of building.

All scholars agree that Solomon extended the City of David mainly to the north. He brought within the city walls the site of the threshing floor of the Jebusite city, which David had bought from the last ruler of Jebus, Ornan or Araunah. In the narrow neck of the ridge connecting the City of David with the extension, Solomon created an area known as *Millo*-"Filling," where he built a palace. The main buildings were erected north of the *Millo*: a great royal house complete with throne room, guard houses, stables, lodgings for the court officials and, in a separate court, the women's quarters.

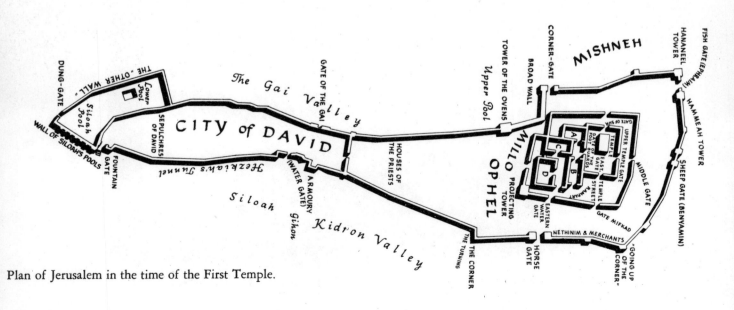

Plan of Jerusalem in the time of the First Temple.

These are believed to be the Tombs of the House of David in the City of David.

The ancient wall of the City of David.

The "Ophel Ostracon" from the
period of the Kingdom of Judah,
containing a list of names in ancient Hebrew script.

The Valley of Jehoshaphat. (See p. 33). Left: the village of Siloam. Right foreground: structure covering the Spring of Gihon which was the main water source of ancient Jerusalem. Here the young Solomon was anointed king (I Kings 1:33, 38).

Typical Israelite altar with "horns" (I Kings 1:50; 2:28).

Reconstruction of the Temple of Solomon—
the First Temple.

Interior of the tunnel cut by King Hezekiah to carry the waters of Gihon into the city when Sennacherib King of Assyria threatened it (II Chronicles 2:30; 33:14).

Inscription in ancient Hebrew describing the cutting of Hezekiah's tunnel and the meeting of the two work gangs which had been digging towards each other.

THE INSCRIPTION READS:

(was completed) the piercing. And this is the story of the piercing. While (the hewers were lifting)
their axes one man against his companion and while three cubits remained to pierce (there was heard) the voice of one man
calling to his companion, for there was a crevice in the rock to the right and left. And on the day of the piercing
the hewers struck one man against his companion, axe against axe, and the waters went
from the spring to the pool two hundred and thousand cubits. And one hundred cubits was the height of the rock above the head of the hewers.
Hezekiah the son of Qara the son of Shoresh the son of Buqiyahu
Ahiyahu the son of Hashoreq the son of Amaqyahu the son of . . .
. . . yahu the son of Qari the son of Amoqyahu the son of . . .

Here the two work gangs met.

By all accounts, Solomon pursued a policy of diplomatic marriages with great persistence. He thus allied himself not only with the Egyptian Pharaoh, but also with the Ammonite, Moabite and Hittite royal families. As a result, the pure spiritual atmosphere which had prevailed in Jerusalem in David's time—his few lapses excepted—degenerated considerably during Solomon's reign.

Yet, even from the religious point of view Solomon served Jerusalem well. By building the magnificent First Temple, he created "a settled place" for God "to abide in forever." The Temple was modelled partly on the Tabernacle (Exodus 25) and partly on Canaanite and Syrian temples of the period. In size, the Temple was not especially overwhelming. Its execution and appurtenances, however—including the copper columns and the copper "sea" (a huge reservoir), made it one of the wonders of the time. Although originally a mere annex of the palace, the Temple soon acquired a life of its own, going on to play a decisive role in the life of the city.

David my servant may have a light always before Me in Jerusalem

I Kings 11:36

JERUSALEM IN THE DIVIDED MONARCHY

The lavish court life and the splendors of the Temple were dearly bought with the forced labor which Solomon imposed on all the tribes but Judah. The slowly accumulated anger of the people erupted as soon as the old king died and an inexperienced youth, his son Rehoboam, mounted the throne. The Ten Tribes of Israel renounced Jerusalem's rule and the city found itself reduced to the capital of the small Kingdom of Judah, comprising but two tribes: Judah and Benjamin.

The first century following the division of the monarchy was a period of decline for Jerusalem. Hard pressed on the north by the more powerful Kingdom of Israel, threatened with the revolt of Edom and thus with the loss of the connection with the Red Sea port of Eilat, harassed by Egyptian invaders, the Kingdom of Judah was hard put merely to keep alive. She had derived one benefit from Israel's secession: many of the priests and levites of Israel, disgusted with the setting up by Jeroboam King of Israel of rival sanctuaries at Dan and Bethel, left the northern kingdom to settle in and around Jerusalem, and thereby enriched the religious life of the capital. The survival of the Davidic dynasty in Jerusalem focussed the loyalty of the people and ensured at least some continuation of the city's role as a spiritual and political center.

From the time of King Jehoshaphat (871-849 B.C.) to the time of Joash (837-789 B.C.) the city recovered somewhat. Judah and Israel made peace and, under the influence of the powerful house of Omri, cultural and commercial ties were established with the Phoenicians. Economic conditions improved and the threat of religious assimilation, which had grown during the reigns of Ahaziah and Athaliah, was eliminated in the palace revolution which established Joash as King and the High Priest Jehoiada as Regent. For the first time now the Temple priesthood established itself as a major factor in the life of Jerusalem.

The city's fortunes reached a new low during the reign of Amaziah (798-784 B.C.), when Jehoash of Israel captured the city and breached its walls from the Gate of Ephraim to the Corner Gate (II Kings 14:13). Under the next two kings, Uzziah and Jotham, however, there was a decisive turn for the better. Allied with Israel, Uzziah re-established Judean sway in the Negev down to Eilat. The renewed prosperity of the Kingdom of Judah under Uzziah was reflected, among other things, in the towers he built at Jerusalem's Corner Gate and Valley Gate and the "engines made by cunning men, to be upon the towers and upon the bulwarks, to shoot arrows and great stones withal" (II Chronicles 26:9, 15). Some scholars believe that the royal palace and the fortress recently excavated at Ramat Rahel, about three miles south of ancient Jerusalem, were built by Uzziah.

The reign of Ahaz, Jotham's son, was marked by two events of far-reaching importance. The Assyrian ascendancy in the ancient Orient began to be felt in Jerusalem, leading to a rise of idolatrous influences and an aping of the Assyrian cult ceremonial which penetrated even to the Temple. At

Sennacherib rides his chariot standing. He is the king of
Assyria who besieged Jerusalem in 701 B.C. (see II Kings
18-19; Ishaiah 36-37; II Chronicles 32.)

the same time, the voice of the first of the great Prophets, Isaiah the son
of Amoz, began to be heard in Jerusalem. Prophecy, in both its social and
moral aspects, went on to become a determinant factor in the life of the
city.

The practical effects of Isaiah's activity were first felt in the reign of Hezekiah (727-698 B.C.). His political firmness, which bolstered the morale
of the people, helped to save Jerusalem during the siege of Sennacherib
in the year 701; and his spiritual zeal led to the first religious reforms.
These reforms continued throughout the period of the Monarchy, with a
temporary lapse in the reign of Menasseh, and culminated in the Great
Reform of Josiah which banished idolatry from Jerusalem for all time.

Materially, the second half of the eighth and the first half of the seventh
centuries B.C. were a period of steady advance. Extensive construction
projects were initiated which required great engineering skill, some of
them necessitated by the precarious security situation. Threatened by Assyria, Hezekiah prepared for a siege. Among other things, he closed the
Gihon spring from the outside and cut a tunnel through the hill of the
City of David which carried the waters of Gihon into a pool in the Central
Valley. An inscription found inside the tunnel proudly describes the meeting of the two digging parties, the length of the tunnel and the work.
Menasseh reinforced the city walls (II Chronicles 33:14). Both Hezekiah

and his great-grandson Josiah spent great sums in repairing the Temple and they stored up considerable treasures.

The great men of the court also initiated important projects. Outstanding among these was the construction of an elaborate set of tombs for the nobles in the Kidron Valley. One of these tombs, with a long inscription mentioning a "royal steward," is believed to be the tomb of Shebna mentioned in Isaiah 22:15.

Now the diversion of the waters of Gihon from the Kidron Valley into the Central Valley has raised an important problem, on whose solution archeologists have not yet agreed—that is, the extent of the city of Jerusalem after the time of Solomon. As we have seen, there is no disagreement as to the location of the Temple north of David's city. But whether Solomon, or some later king, extended the city walls to include the western hill—which is now popularly but erroneously known as Mount Zion—is in much dispute. In any case, the making of a pool inside the Central Valley must imply that that area was within the walls. For otherwise, the whole project would have been senseless. Perhaps the account of Hezekiah's building "another wall without" (II Chronicle 32:5) refers to a wall encircling the pool. As yet no excavations and no writings have been found which would conclusively prove that "Mount Zion" was a part of the city of Jerusalem in that period.

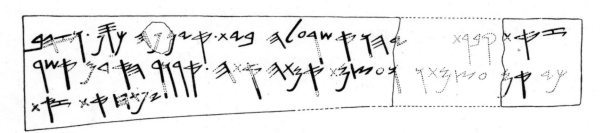

Tomb inscription in Hebrew from about the 7th century B.C. It reads:
Line 1:   This is (the sepulchre of . . .)yahu who is over the house. There is no silver and no gold here
Line 2:   but (his bones) and the bones of his slave-wife with him. Cursed be the man
Line 3:   who will open this.

16. set him on the royal throne over them and
17. imposed upon him my kingly tribute.
18. As for Hezekiah, the Jew,
19. who did not submit to my yoke, 46 of his strong, walled cities, as well as
20. the small cities in their neighborhood,
21. which were without number,—by levelling with battering-rams(?)
22. and by bringing up siege-engines(?), by attacking and storming on foot,
23. by mines, tunnels and breaches(?), I besieged and took (those cities).
24. 200,150 people, great and small, male and female,
25. horses, mules, asses, camels,
26. cattle and sheep, without number, I brought away from them
27. and counted as spoil. Himself, like a caged bird
28. I shut up in Jerusalem his royal city.
29. Earthworks I threw up against him,—
30. the one coming out of the city-gate, I turned back to his misery.
31. The cities of his, which I had despoiled, I cut off from his land and
32. to Mitinti, king of Ashdod,
33. Padi, king of Ekron, and Silli-bêl
34. king of Gaza, I gave. And (thus) I diminished his land.
35. I added to the former tribute,
36. and laid upon him the giving (up) of their land, (as well as) imposts—gifts for my majesty.
37. As for Hezekiah,
38. the terrifying splendor of my majesty overcame him, and
39. the Urbi (Arabs) and his mercenary(?) troops which he had brought in to strengthen
40. Jerusalem, his royal city,
41. deserted him (lit. took leave). In addition to the 30 talents of gold and
42. 800 talents of silver, (there were) gems, antimony,
43. jewels(?), large *sandu*-stones, couches of ivory,
44. house-chairs of ivory, elephant hide, ivory (lit. elephant's "teeth")
45. ebony(?), boxwood(?), all kinds of valuable (heavy) treasures,
46. as well as his daughters, his harem, his male and female
47. musicians, (which) he had (them) bring after me
48. to Nineveh, my royal city. To pay tribute
49. and to accept (lit. do) servitude, he dispatched his messengers.
50. In my fourth campaign Assur, my lord, gave me courage, and
51. I mustered my numerous armies and gave the
52. command to proceed against Bît-Yakin. In the course of my campaign
53. I accomplished the overthrow of Shuzubi, the Chaldean,—who sat in the midst of the swamps,—
54. at Bitûtu.
55. That one,—the terror (lit. ague, chills) of my battle fell upon him, and

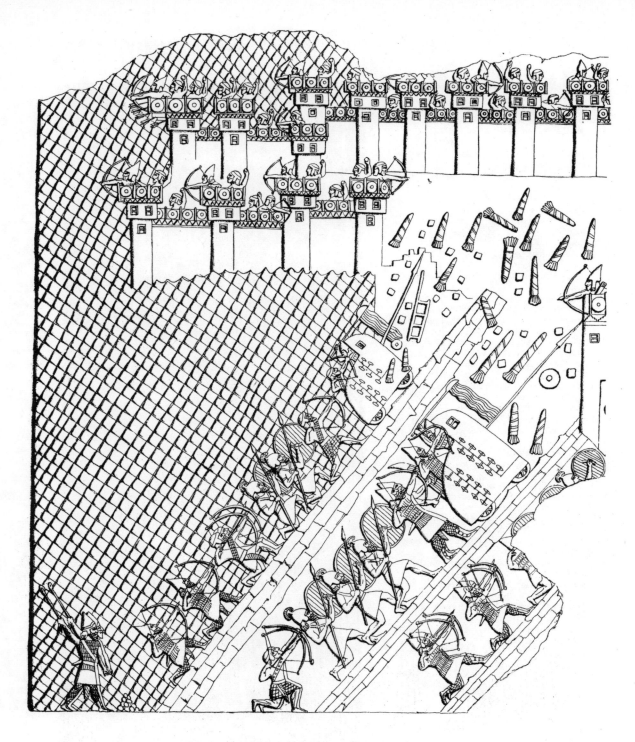

Assyrian tablet depicting the siege of a Judean city. Atop the city walls are structures resembling the "machines" of Uzziah King of Judah (II Chronicles 26:15).

How doth the city sit solitary, that was full of people

Lamentations 1:1

Jerusalem escaped the Assyrian peril, which had proved fatal to its sister, Samaria, capital of the Kingdom of Israel. But the political turmoil which followed the fall of the Assyrian Empire marked the decline of the City and Dynasty of David.

The feverish maneuvers of the last kings of Judah are enough proof that they were in an untenable position between the conflicting aspirations of the great powers of the period. Josiah, the religious reformer, fell at Megiddo helping Babylon to defend herself against Egypt. In 597, Nebuchadnezzar King of Babylon exiled King Jehoiachin together with a great portion of the upper classes and the craftsmen of Jerusalem.

Zedekiah, the last King of Judah, vacillated between the agitation of the war party and the Prophet Jeremiah's counsel of appeasement. Finally, in 586 B.C., after a siege of several months—good proof of the strength of the city's fortifications—Jerusalem fell. Zedekiah was captured as he tried to flee through the gate between the two walls while the Babylonian princes sat in the Middle Gate north of the Temple. Finally Nebuzaradan, an envoy of Nebuchadnezzar, "burnt the house of the Lord and the king's house and all the houses of Jerusalem" (II Kings 25:9).

Thus ended another chapter in the history of Jerusalem.

Typical Israelite dress of
the 8th-7th centuries B.C.

If I forget thee, Jerusalem, may my right hand
lose its cunning

Psalms 137:5

THE BABYLONIAN CAPTIVITY AND THE FIRST RETURN TO ZION

The Land of Judah became the property of the conqueror. The Babylonian Royal Captain of the Guard left only "the poor of the land to be vine-dressers and husbandmen" (II Kings 25:12) and Jerusalem ceased to exist politically. Yet, though desolate, the Holy City remained the exclusive property of the Jews and continued to function as their religious center. From Jeremiah 41:5 we learn that offerings continued to be brought to the House of God even after its destruction. What is more, the Babylonians never carried out a policy of mass population resettlement as the Assyrians had done with the Ten Tribes of Israel.

In the Babylonian exile, where the Jews quickly established themselves commercially, agriculturally and religiously, the memory of Jerusalem was kept alive by the prophets and poets. Thus, when Cyrus, King of Persia, conquered the Babylonian empire and issued a decree allowing the Jews to rebuild the Temple, a small but substantial number of the exiles returned to Jerusalem. The rulers of Samaria tried in every way to hinder the rebuilding of the Temple and the re-establishment of the city as the capital of a province not dependent on them. The reconstruction of the city therefore proceeded slowly and each of the four waves of immigration which came following Cyrus' decree over a period of nearly five generations was called upon to perform at least one of four major tasks in the city's recovery. These tasks were: the re-establishment of Jerusalem's autonomy; the reconstruction of the Temple; the repair of the city walls, which had been breached but left standing; and the consolidation of the nation's spiritual values.

First came Sheshbazzar, a prince of the line of David. He and his followers established sacrificial worship. More important was the second wave of immigration, led by Zerubavel, who was appointed Governor of Judah, and the High Priest Joshua, son of Yehozedek. In 515 B.C., 71 years after

Lane in the Old City. Left is the foundation of one of the towers of the Fortress of Antonia.

The "Wailing Wall" is a relic of the western wall of the Second Temple as rebuilt by Herod. The Moslems and Christians gave it its present name, because the Jews used to make pilgrimages here to bewail the destruction of the Temple.

This pillar, resting where it was originally cut into the rock on the site of the ancient quarry in the Russian Compound, is believed to have been cut by Herod for his basilica at the southern end of the Temple Mount. It apparently was abandoned by the masons when it cracked.

55

The springing of "Robinson's Arch," which was built by Herod. With "Wilson's Arch" (see p. 43), this was one of the two arches connecting the Temple Mount to the Upper City.

Rosette carved on an ossuary of the Second Temple period.

Old City lane leading to the "Wailing Wall."

Reconstruction of the Tombs of the Kings.

Staircase of the Tombs of the Kings. Right are channels leading to the purification cisterns at the entrance.

Facade of the Tombs of the Kings.
Here lie buried the family of Queen
Helena of Adiabene (Mesopotamia), who came to Jerusalem with
her children in about A.D. 45 and
converted to Judaism.

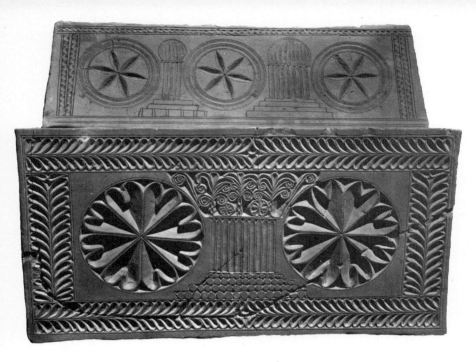

Richly ornamented ossuary of
the Second Temple period.

Tomb of the family of Nicanor, an Alexandrian
Jew who had contributed elegant doors to the
Second Temple. Many ossuaries were found in
the tomb, one bearing Nicanor's name. In this
photograph, taken from the entrance, the ossuaries rest exactly as they were first found.

it was destroyed, Zerubavel and Joshua restored the Temple. The Prophet Haggai declared that the Second Temple was as nothing compared to the First, but that "the glory of this latter house shall be greater than of the the former" (2:9). Soon afterwards, Zerubavel disappears from the stage of history and, with a few exceptions, it was the High Priest who henceforth ruled Jerusalem. Thus the priesthood finally freed itself from the several centuries of control by the Royal House of David.

The wall of Jerusalem also is broken down and the gates thereof are burned with fire

Nehemiah 1:3

THE RESTORATION OF THE WALLS

In view of its many enemies, Jerusalem could not pursue an independent course so long as its walls were breached and its gates open to every would-be assailant. It was Nehemiah the son of Hakhaliah, a high Persian Court officer, who provided the material base for the reorganization of the Jewish Commonwealth. In 440 B.C. he was appointed Governor of Jerusalem. Coming to the city, he personally checked the walls and then had them repaired, undaunted by the threats of his enemies. Their morale high, the people enthusiastically completed the work in 52 days. "Everyone with one of his hands wrought in the work and with the other hand held a weapon" (Nehemiah 4:17). Nehemiah's account of the project gives us the first detailed description of the limits of ancient Jerusalem and is the base for every attempt to reconsruct an image of the city.
Nehemiah also ordered all the nobles and one tenth of the village population to move into Jerusalem and declared a moratorium on unjust debts, which had reduced the peasants of Judah to virtual serfdom.

Once Judah was fortified materially, Ezra the Scribe (about 428 B.C.) could proceed with his spiritual reform and to establish the Rule of the Law. The Temple was purified, mixed marriages dissolved and the class of Scribes—experts in Mosaic Law—now acquired equal status with the nobility and priesthood. The Scribes established Jerusalem once and for all as the undisputed spiritual center of Judah and the entire Jewish Diaspora in Egypt, Babylonia and Asia Minor.

HELLENISTIC RULE (333-168 B.C.)

With Ezra and Nehemiah, the Biblical Period comes to an end. New forces arose in the world and the struggle for the preservation of Jerusalem's spiritual integrity took a different turn.

The beginnings of Hellenistic rule in the Holy Land were peaceful. The people, led by the High Priest Yaddua, submitted without a struggle to Alexander the Great, who, at the same time, did not molest them. In the struggle among Alexander's successors over the division of his empire, however, Jerusalem fell in 312 B.C. to Ptolemy I Soter, King of Egypt. He deported part of the city's population to Alexandria, but confirmed the remainder in their autonomy and the validity of the traditional laws. He left the city in the charge of a garrison of Egyptian troops who were probably stationed in the Fortress Baris adjoining the Temple on the north.

For all the apparent conservatism and moderation of Hellenistic rule, the new philosophy began to gain Jewish adherents, especially among the aristocracy and even some of the younger priests. A factor in this growing spiritual ferment were the Seleucid rulers of Syria, who laid claim to Palestine and tried to conquer it by force or intrigue, nurturing the division between the adherents of the old culture and the new. At this time, economic struggles began to play their part in dividing the nation. After

A detail of "Wilson's Arch", the bridge built during the Hasmonean period to connect the Temple Mount with the Upper City.

Detail of wall found in the Citadel of Jerusalem (traditionally called the "Tower of David") which is believed to have been built by the Hasmoneans.

General view of tombs in the Valley of Jehoshaphat from the Second Temple period. Left: the so-called "Pillar" or "Tomb of Absalom" (see II Samuel 18:18-19); center: the tomb of the priestly family of Hezir; right: the traditional "Tomb of the Prophet Zechariah."

This coin was issued by Mattathias Antigonus (40-37 B.C.), the last of the Hasmonean rulers.

This coin, issued by Antiochus VII Sidetes (138-129 B.C.), may have been minted in Jerusalem.

Southeast corner of the wall of the Temple Mount from Herod's time.

Entrance to the Citadel of Jerusalem. Right is the foundation of the Tower of Phasael, one of the three towers which defended Herod's palace on the north.

The wall of the Temple Mount, looking at the Mosque el-Aqsa from the south. The recesses in the wall at the right are remnants of the Temple wall.

"Court of the Prison," the traditional site of the dungeon where the Prophet Jeremiah was imprisoned (Jeremiah 38:6). It served as a fosse before the second wall of ancient Jerusalem.

centuries of slow growth under the Persians, Jerusalem began to rise rapidly in the time of general prosperity which characterized the early Hellenistic period. The Temple was still Judah's banking and business center, but rich and noble families in the favor of the Egyptian Ptolemaic court began to vie for economic predominance. In exchange for a lump payment, the king allowed them to farm the country's taxes.

After several attempts, Antiochus III, King of Syria, ousted the Ptolemies from Palestine in 198 B.C. The Jerusalemites supplied him and helped him to take the Baris citadel from the Egyptian garrison. In gratitude, Antiochus granted Judah a charter allowing the Jews to live according to their traditional customs. The Temple priests and scribes were exempted from taxes forever and the Jerusalem civilian population for three years, and it was forbidden to bring into Jerusalem ritually impure animals or even their hides.

This charter remained in force till the time of his son and successor, Antiochus IV Epiphanes, during whose reign the Hasmonean Revolt took place. The younger Antiochus inherited a heavy burden of tribute imposed on his father after his defeat by the Romans. To pay this tribute and to consolidate his kingdom, Antiochus impounded the treasures of the various temples and started to hellenize the oriental religions in his empire. In Jerusalem he had the help of part of the priesthood, one of whom, Menelaus, he appointed High Priest, though he was not legally qualified, thus abrogating his father's charter. When the defeated candidate attacked Jerusalem while Antiochus was campaigning against Egypt, the furious king went up to Jerusalem and occupied it. The Altar was desecrated and the Temple converted into a Hellenistic sanctuary. In the face of growing resistance, the king grew increasingly violent. He garrisoned the city and built a fortress opposite the Temple to hold it in submission. A new city, to be called Antioch, was planned on the broad western hill. The practice of Judaism was banned under penalty of death. Many patriots fled to the wilderness or to provincial towns. It was in one of these towns that the liberation movement was sparked.

THE HASMONEANS: REVOLT AND RULE

MATTATHIAS THE HASMONEAN

The revolt was set off by a priest of Modiin, Mattathias the Hasmonean, when he refused to sacrifice to alien gods. His son Judah, nicknamed *Hamakkabi,* "The Hammer," became its military leader. In the first years of the struggle, Jerusalem—although held by a garrison of Syrian troops and hellenized Jews—was the pivot of operations. Judah set out to cut its communications with the plain, so as to isolate it. After defeating four Syrian armies in as many pitched battles on the approaches to the city at Levonah, Beit Horon, Emmaus and Beit Zur, Judah took the Temple Mount in 164 B.C. He immediately purified the Temple and restored the worship—a joyous event which has been commemorated in the Festival of Hanukah.

For 23 years Jerusalem was divided between the Temple Mount, which was largely controlled by the Jews, and the Fortress of Acra opposite, the stronghold of the hellenizers. Even within the Temple, power passed from time to time to the opponents of the Hasmoneans. Finally the Hasmoneans prevailed. In 152 B.C. Jonathan, a brother of Judah Hamakkabi, was appointed High Priest and Governor of Judah. Jonathan was thus, in fact, an independent ruler. In 141 B.C., Simon, Jonathan's brother and successor, took Acra and Jerusalem remained wholly Jewish till its destruction by the Roman Titus in 70 A.D.

For all their successes, the Hasmoneans were not safe from attack. Energetic kings of Syria, notably Antiochus VII Sidetes, assaulted Jerusalem and exercised the right of coinage there. To meet this danger, the city's walls were strengthened, and the western hill was now included for probably the first time in the city's defenses. Part of the Acra fortress was destroyed and the rest was turned into a residence for the Hasmonean rulers.

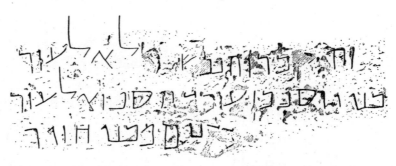

Inscription on the facade of the tomb of the priestly family of Hezir: "This is the tomb and monument of Elazar Hanaiah Yoezer Yehuda Shimon Yohanan the sons of Yosef son of Oved (and) Yosef and Elazar the sons of Hanaiah Priests of the Bene Hezir."

Moses reading the Torah—Fresco found in the Dura-Europos Synagogue in Mesopotamia, showing the typical appearance and dress of a Jerusalemite of the Hellenistic-Roman period.

Facade of the "Cave of the Sanhedrin" or "Tombs of the Judges," dating from the late Second Temple period.

Remnants of a double gate at the south wall of the Temple Mount.

Section of an aqueduct which carried water to Jerusalem from the Bethlehem area. It was built by Pontius Pilate with Temple funds.

The rock in the Dome of the Rock at the center of the Temple Mount. Some scholars believe it to have been the site of the Temple's Holy of Holies; others say the Great Altar was located here. This is the rock on which Abraham is believed to have been prepared to sacrifice Isaac and from which Mohammed is said to have ascended into Heaven.

Capital from the fortress built by the Kings of Judah in the 8th century B.C. near modern Ramat Rahel.

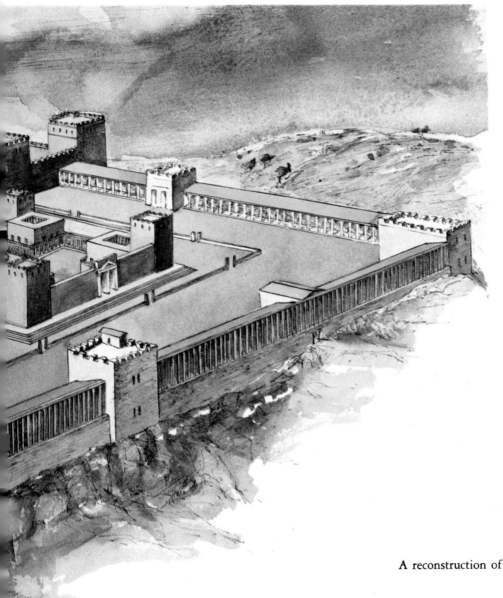

A reconstruction of the Second Temple.

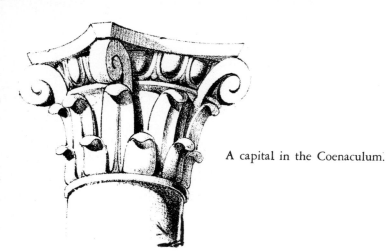

A capital in the Coenaculum.

The Coenaculum, believed to be the site of the Last Supper. This hall is part of a Crusader church built on Mount Zion in the 12th century.

The Temple Mount—In the foreground is the Wailing Wall.

"Pool of Bethesda"—Here Jesus is
believed to have healed the cripple
(John 5).

By 76 B.C. Jerusalem was once more the headquarters of an expanding kingdom enjoying suzerainty over almost the whole of the historic Land of Israel, instead of being the capital of a minor Seleucid province. Attempts to transfer the center of Jewish worship elsewhere failed miserably. Now that Jerusalem and Judah were at peace, the pilgrimage movement increased and was reflected in the growing prosperity of the city. Evidence of this exists in the series of monuments and rock-cut tombs that in the Kidron Valley, such as the Tomb of the Benei Hezir and the so-called Tomb of Zechariah (see illustrations).

The Hasmonean revolt began as a reaction against the hellenizing tendency among the Jews. Once the revolt had succeeded and the Hasmoneans established themselves as the rulers of Judah, they soon learned that no state could exist in that period without absorbing some elements of Greek culture. Thus we find a strong influence of Greek architecture—the Doric and Ionic columns, the frieze of triglyphs and metopes, etc.—in the tombs of the rich Jerusalemites who could afford mausoleums.

On their coins the Hasmoneans, while trying to imitate the coinage of the period, as a rule avoided offensive images. Thus they adopted the two cornucopias but replaced the pagan caduceus between them with a poppy blossom; and they replaced the image of the ruler with a long inscription in ancient Hebrew script. Only in the coins of the last Hasmonean, Mattatyahu Antigonos (40-37 B.C.), does a definitely Jewish element appear. These coins show the seven-branched Temple candelabrum, which was made anew by Judah Hamakkabi when he purified the Temple, on one side and the shewbread table on the other.

Throughout this period there was a constant tug-of-war between the Saducees, the wealthy and hellenizing ruling party, and the Pharisees, the rabbinical party which had the backing of the masses. In addition to the economic and cultural basis of this struggle, there was the fact that the Hasmoneans, who were priests, had committed a serious breach of tradition by assuming the throne. The rabbis and masses had never reconciled themselves to this usupation of the Crown of Kingdom by those who were supposed to wear only the Crown of Priesthood. This conflict assumed bloodbath proportitions during the reign of Alexander Jannaeus (103-

76), at a time when the borders of the Jewish State were as far extended as they have ever been.

This civil war between the Saducees and the Pharisees broke out anew under Alexander's quarreling sons, Aristobulus II and Hyrcanus II. The war led first to the siege of Jerusalem by the forces of the Nabataean King Aretas, who came to the aid of Hyrcanus, and then to the intervention of the Roman general Pompey (63 B. C.). During Pompey's siege the city was divided both spiritually and physically. The Upper City was in the hands of Hyrcanus and his followers while Aristobulus and his partisans beld the Temple. The big fosse north of the Temple and the bridge ("Wilson's Arch," as its remains are called after the man who discovered them in the 19th century—see illustrations) connecting the Temple Mount with the Upper City are now mentioned for the first time. In the end, of course, Roman siegecraft and military power prevailed. The Temple was stormed but its treasures left intact; it was another Roman general, Crassus, who confiscated them some years later. Pompey breached the walls and installed Hyrcanus as nominal Ethnarch and High Priest. The real power, however, passed to Antipater and his family, descendants of Edomites who had been forcibly converted to Judaism by the Hasmoneans some years earlier. It was one of Antipater's sons, Herod, who by the favor of Rome unseated the Hasmoneans and established his own dynasty.

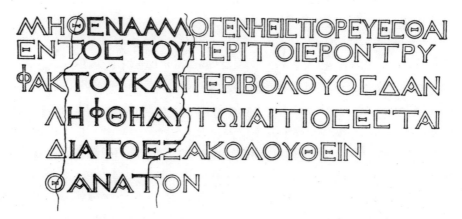

Inscription forbidding Gentiles to pass the partition surrounding the Inner Temple.

KING HEROD AND HIS TEMPLE

Herod secured Jerusalem as his capital after a long siege in which Mattatyahu Antigonos, the last Hasmonean, and most of the old aristocracy
perished. In the Temple Herod placed priestly families who were obedient
to him in the hope of obtaining the High Priesthood by his favor. As an
obedient vassal of Rome, Herod was able to expand his territory till it
comprised almost the entire Holy Land. The country was divided into
two almost equal parts—the Greek cities and the non-Jewish countryside,
and the Jewish section with Jerusalem as its center.

The country prospered under Herod. The pacification of the Roman
world by the Emperor Augustus and the resultant prosperity led to a
renewal of the pilgrimage movement from the Diaspora to Jerusalem and
a great increase in the contribution of the Jews of the Diaspora to the
Temple and, indirectly, for the Holy City. This, combined with Herod's
efficiency as a tax collector and astuteness as a businessman, enabled him
to embark on a great program of reconstruction and new building in
Jerusalem and throughout the country.

Herod's activity in Jerusalem was, like most of his policies, two-faced.
On the one hand, aware that he was despised by the rabbis and much of
the masses, and in almost paranoic fear for his safety, he went about
fortifying his position in the city. He built a citadel-palace at the northwestern end of the Upper City. This grandiose structure and its gardens
were protected by a wall with towers. Especially famous are the three
towers on the north, named for Herod's brother, wife and friend: Phasael,
Miriam and Hippicus. The stump of the largest tower, Phasael, still
stands and is popularly known as "The Tower of David." The wisdom of
Herod's choice of a site for his palaces is evidenced in the fact that all
subsequent rulers of Jerusalem located their citadels on the same spot.
To secure the Temple he built the Fortress Antonia—named for Mark
Antony—at the northwestern corner of the Temple Mount on the site
of the ancient Fortress Baris.

At the same time, Herod also "rendered unto God" and popular feeling by rebuilding the Temple. Even the rabbis, no friends of his, had to concede that "Who has not beheld the Temple of Herod has never seen beauty in his life" (Talmud Tractate *Baba Batra* 3b). Architecturally, the Temple conformed to the style of the time. Ritually, tradition was strictly observed.

To even out the whole Temple area, Herod built a huge esplanade, part of whose outer walls still stand. The Valley of Tyropoeion was deflected from its course and another bridge (today known as "Robinson's Arch" after its discoverer) was built, connecting the Temple Mount with the Upper City. On the south side of the Temple Mount a beautiful basilica was erected. The Inner Temple, which constituted a fortress within a fortress, was surrounded by a balustrade with inscriptions warning Gentiles not to cross it on pain of death (see illustration). Within the Temple, the Women's Court with its four subsidiary courts was entered by an exquisite gate called "The Beautiful" (Acts 3:10). The gate leading to the inner court was contributed by Nicanor, an Alexandrian Jew, whose family tomb was found some time ago near the Hebrew University campus on Mt. Scopus (see illustration). In the center of the inner court stood the Sanctuary, with its 150-foot-high facade of marble and gold gleaming so that it appeared from afar as a "mountain of snow glittering in the sun."

Apart from the remains of the Temple, the most resplendent monuments left from the Herodian era are a great number of mausoleums and tombs such as the Family Tomb of Herod with its rolling stone, the Tombs of the Kings, the so-called "Tomb of Absalom" and the so-called "Tombs of the Judges" (see illustrations). In none of them are to be found human or animal images. All of them, however, are rich in floral ornament.

Garden of Gethsemane—The ancient olive grove in the Valley of Jehoshaphat, at the foot of the Mount of Olives, where Jesus passed the night before being arrested by the High Priest. In the left background are the city wall and the Golden Gate.

The Via Dolorosa—On the left is
the Seventh Station, where St. Ve-
ronica dried Jesus' face.

General view of the Church of the Holy Sepulchre.

Belfry Tower of the Church of the Holy Sepulchre. A remnant of Crusader days.

Courtyard and facade of the Church of the Holy Sepulchre, which date from the time of the Crusaders. The staircase at the right leads up to Calvary.

Edicule of the Holy Sepulchre.

Entrance to "Herod's Cave," near the Y.M.C.A. in the New City. Here are the remains of an ancient mausoleum, faced with big stones, in which members of Herod's family are believed to have been buried. The entrance was blocked up by the rolling stone shown above, similar to the one which sealed Jesus' tomb. (See Mark 15:46; 27:60.)

Coin showing head of Agrippa I, King of Judah (37-44 A.D.), before whom Paul spoke in Caesarea (Acts 25:13-26:32).

This mosque, formerly a church, stands on the traditional site of the Ascension on the Mount of Olives.

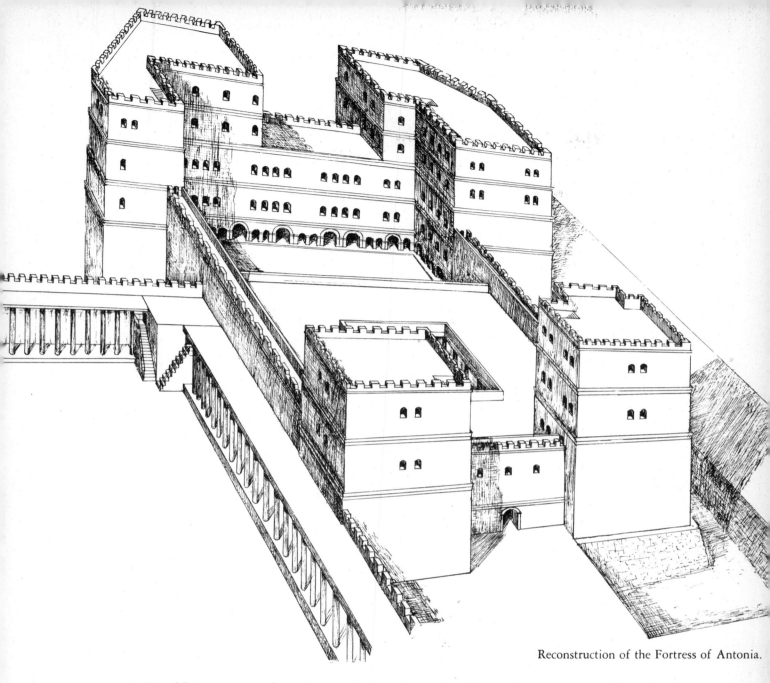

Reconstruction of the Fortress of Antonia.

In addition, scores of smaller tombs have been found around Jerusalem, containing burial niches cut into the rock and filled with ossuaries. These are small limestone boxes in which bones were interred. They are decorated in a semi-geometric style, with rosettes drawn with a compass and carved into the soft stone with a knife. The Greek and Aramaic inscriptions on the ossuaries are a major source of information as to the ethnic composition of Jerusalem and the names used by Jerusalemites before its destruction in 70 A. D.

Candelabrum of the Second Temple as depicted in the Arch of Titus in Rome. The Arch, built after Titus' death in 81, has two reliefs depicting his triumphal march after the capture of Jerusalem.

JESUS

For nine years after Herod died, Judah was ruled ineptly by his son Archelaus (4 B. C.-6 A. D.). He was deposed and thenceforth the city and country were ruled by Roman procurators, except during the three-year reign (41-44 A.D.) of Herod's grandson, Agrippa I. Jerusalem in effect ceased to be a capital when the Roman governors established their residence at Caesarea on the Mediterranean coast. This humiliation, the extortionate conduct of the officialdom and the presence in the Antonia fortress of a Roman garrison which guarded the High Priestly vestments kept the country in constant ferment. It was during the regime of one of these governors, Pontius Pilate (26-36 A.D.), that Jerusalem was the scene of one of the most important events in its history, comparable in its after-effects only with the conquest of David and the erection of the Temple by Solomon. This was the mission and death of Jesus.

According to the New Testament, which is the only source for the events in his career, the infant Jesus was brought to the Temple after his circumcision and was again in Jerusalem at the age of 12, during a Pilgrimage festival. He returned to the Temple on three Passovers, traditionally assigned to the years 27, 28 and 30; again on the Feast of Sukkot (Tabernacles) in 29 and two months later during the Festival of Hanukah. His visits to Jerusalem are marked by various healings, such as that of the cripple at the pool of Bethesda north of the Temple, and some major doctrinal pronouncements. The Passover week of the year 30 was especially memorable. Jesus made a triumphal entry into the city from the Mount of Olives through the East Gate (probably situated where St. Stephen's Gate stands today). He was received by part of the population waving palm branches and chanting "Hosanna." He did not lodge in the city, however, but at Bethany on the Mount of Olives, the residence of the family of Lazarus, Martha and Mary Magdalene. On Passover day, Jesus sent two disciples into the city to prepare for the feast. He followed in the evening with the rest of the disciples, observing the prescribed *Seder* rite, in connection with which Jesus uttered the eucharistic blessings. The locale of this *Seder*—the Last Supper—is not indicated in the Gospels. Tradition, however, places it in the Coenaculum, a hall above the so-called "Tomb of David" on Mt. Zion, which was then considered the aristocratic quarter of the Upper City.

After the Last Supper, Jesus and the disciples retired to the Garden of Gethsemane at the foot of the Mount of Olives. "Gethsemane" is the Greek form of the Hebrew *"gat shemanim,"* meaning "oil press," and is undoubtedly connected with the abundance of olive groves which then covered the slopes of the mountain inclining towards the Kidron Valley. Some ancient olive trees still standing in the area are believed to have been there in the time of Jesus. In was in Gethsemane that Jesus was arrested and brought by the Captain of the Temple, the officer in charge of the building's security, to the house of the High Priest Caiaphas. Tradition places this building a short distance from the Coenaculum, in the then Upper City. After a brief interrogation, Jesus was declared to be a blasphemer, subject to the death penalty. Since the Sanhedrin, the rabbinical court, was not authorized to sentence and execute, Jesus was turned over to Pontius Pilate, who had come to Jerusalem to watch for possible disturbances during the tumultuous Passover season when the city was crowded with pilgrims.

According to tradition, the Roman governor resided at the Antonia fortress. Here, too, are placed the Arch of Ecce Homo ("Behold the Man"—John 19 : 5), where Pontius exhibited Jesus to the populace before the Crucifixion, and the Lithostrotus, the stone pavement of the Praetorium where Jesus was judged. Accordingly, this is the beginning of the Via Dolorosa.

Pontius sent Jesus to the Tetrarch Herod, who was also in the city then, living probably at the Herodian palace inherited from the Hasmoneans and located close to where "Wilson's Arch" joined the Upper City and the Temple Mount. Then sent back to Pontius, Jesus was condemned by the Roman governor as a political offender—having claimed to be "King of the Jews"—and executed by the Roman method of crucifixion.

Tradition places the Crucifixion at a site known today as Golgotha or Calvary and Jesus' burial nearby at the site of the Church of the Holy Sepulchre. For here is believed to be the tomb of Joseph of Arimathea in which Jesus was buried. Joseph, a wealthy Jerusalem counsellor, placed the tomb which he had prepared for himself at the disposal of Jesus' disciples. Several similar tombs, with a rolling stone serving as a door, have been found at the Tomb of Herod's Family and that of the Kings (see illustrations). The site of the tomb has been covered by the rotunda of the Church of the Holy Sepulchre since 335, the time of the Emperor Constantine. Here Christian tradition places the Resurrection. The Ascension 40 days after Easter is placed at the site of a mosque which was formerly the Church of the Ascension on the Mount of Olives.

THE FIRST ROMAN WAR

The political ferment which played a major part in the execution of Jesus did not simmer down. Nationalistic feelings ran high, fanned by the corruption and oppression of the Roman administrative personnel selected to govern Judah and Jerusalem. The only respite was during the three-year reign of the Jewish King Agrippa I.

Matters came to a head in 66, during the regime of the Roman Governor Festus. A band of patriots seized the fortress of Massada on the western shore of the Dead Sea and equipped itself with the arms found in Massada's huge arsenal. Under the leadership of Menahem, they marched on Jerusalem at the time of the Feast of Sukkot, when the city was thronged with pilgrims. In the outbreak that followed, the citadels of the Fortress Antonia and of Herod's Palace were taken after a brief resistance. During the battle, part of the city was burnt down, including the archives containing the hated debt records.

The "Golden Gate" in the east wall of Aelia Capitolina.

A section of the Old City wall built on the foundations of the Roman colony.

Helena, the mother of the Emperor Constantine.

The Chapel of Saint He-
lena in the Church of the
Holy Sepulchre, where the
True Cross was believed
to have been found in
326.

Byzantine mosaic in the Chapel of Golgotha depicting Jesus as Lord of the Universe.

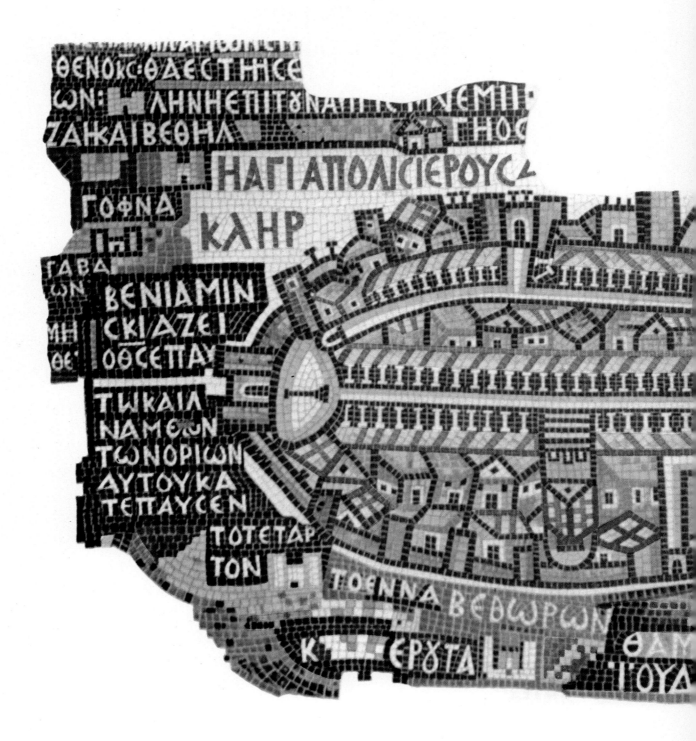

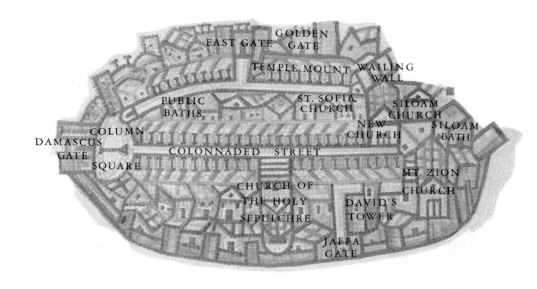

Jerusalem and environs in the Medeba mosaic map.

A monk enters the Greek Orthodox Monastery of the Cross. This monastery was built in the 12th century on the spot where the tree from which the Cross was made was believed to have grown.

In the chapel of the Monastery of the Cross.

Illustration in a Byzantine Christian
manuscript depicting the Nativity,
now in the library of the Greek
Orthodox Patriarchate.

The revolt thus became a revolution. Its original leader, Menahem, was captured and killed while trying to hide in the Ophel Quarter, a district of patriots, but the new leaders, nationalists of the upper class, continued with the war. The nearest Roman army was in Syria, and a long time passed before Cestius Gallus, Governor of Syria and official superior of the Procurator of Judah, appeared in the field with his legions. He penetrated into the city almost to the Temple gates. In the face of stiff resistance, however, and realizing his precarious position in the heart of a hostile country, he decided to withdraw. In his retreat, in the autumn of 66, Cestius was soundly defeated at the Descent of Beit Horon and lost his siege train. The captured engines of war later served the defenders of Jerusalem well.

Till the Passover of 70, the city was secure from Roman attack. During this same period, however, it was rent by internal strife. The revolutionary government of the High Priests was overthrown by the zealots who swarmed to Jerusalem after the Romans took Galilee. These, headed by Yohanan of Gush-Halav (John of Gischala), were in turn threatened by another group of zealots headed by Simon Bar Giora. In the civil war between the two parties—with the occasional intervention of a third—the city's human, material and food resources, enough for many years, were dissipated. The warring factions made peace when Titus, son and heir of the Emperor Vespasian, arrived with an army of four legions. But by now, the city was ill prepared to stand a long siege. It was only the grim determination and resourcefulness of the defenders that enabled them to hold out against Titus for four mounths.

At the time of the Great Siege, a full account of which appears in Josephus' *The Jewish war,* Jerusalem was defended by three main walls. The First or Inner Wall encompassed the southern extremities of the two hills on which the city stood. The northern face of the wall, the only one vulnerable to attack under the conditions of ancient siege warfare, ran from Herod's Three Towers along a small valley running from west to east. Crossing the Central of Tyropoeion Valley, the wall joined the Fortress Antonia and the Temple's northern defenses. Additional protection was provided by two pools: the Amygdalon or Towers Pool (popularly

Coin minted by Vespasian celebrating the suppresion of the Jewish revolt. On the obverse is a bust of Vespasian and a list of his titles. On the reverse, a Jew stands captive on one side of the palm tree, a Jewess sits mourning on the other side, and around them is the legend: IV-DAEA CAPTA (Judea Subjugated).

Coin minted by Hadrian celebrating the establishment of Colonia Aelia Capitolina on the ruins of Jerusalem in 135. The obverse bears the bust of Hadrian and his titles; the reverse shows Hadrian plowing with a bull and a cow, the standard of the Legio Quinta (Fifth Legion) in the background, and the legend COL(onia) AEL(ia) CAPIT(olina).

called the "Pool of Hezekiah") and the pool known in Arabic as *Birket Israin* (the Pool of Israel). Before the First Wall, to the north, stood the Second Wall, which enclosed the commercial quarter in a semi-circle extending from Gennath Gate in the First Wall to the Antonia fortress. The Third or Outer Wall, begun by Agrippa I but abandoned by order of the Romans, was hastily completed by the revolutionary government. It reached the high ground between the Kidron Valley and the Valley of the Son of Hinnom.

Carefully planning his strategy, Titus established his main camp opposite the Three Towers and posted a legion on the Mount of Olives. His original plan was to breach the Outer Wall near the Three Towers, move on to the First Wall and, by taking Herod's Palace and the Upper City, finish the siege at one stroke. The Romans easily breached the Outer Wall, but the rest of the plan was thwarted by the stiff resistance of the forces led by Simon Bar Giora. Titus now decided to fence in the city with a circumvallation wall and starve the inhabitants into submission. The wall passed from the Assyrian Camp (believed to be the present-day Russian Compound in New Jerusalem), where Sennacherib had conducted his siege of Jerusalem in 701 B. C. and where Titus now established his headquarters, down to the Kidron Valley, then to the Rock of the Dovecotes in the Siloam Valley, up to Hanania's Hill, up again to the Family Tomb of Herod and back to the Assyrian Camp. Early in the month of Av (July-August), the assault was renewed against the Fortress Antonia and the Three Towers. In an epic struggle, the Romans were repulsed at the Towers but broke the resistance at Antonia and entered the Temple. On the ninth of Av the Temple was burnt down. Then came the destruction of the Lower City down to the Pool of Siloam. The Upper City, defended by an interior wall, held out about three weeks longer. The victors left the Three Towers standing as a monument to their conquest and as a defense of the legionary camp which they established on the ruins of the palace.

The Land of Judah now became the minor Roman Province of Judea.

Silver shekel of "Year 2" of the "First Jewish War" (67-68 A.D.). The obverse is inscribed "Jerusalem the Holy" and the reverse, "Shekel of Israel Year 2."

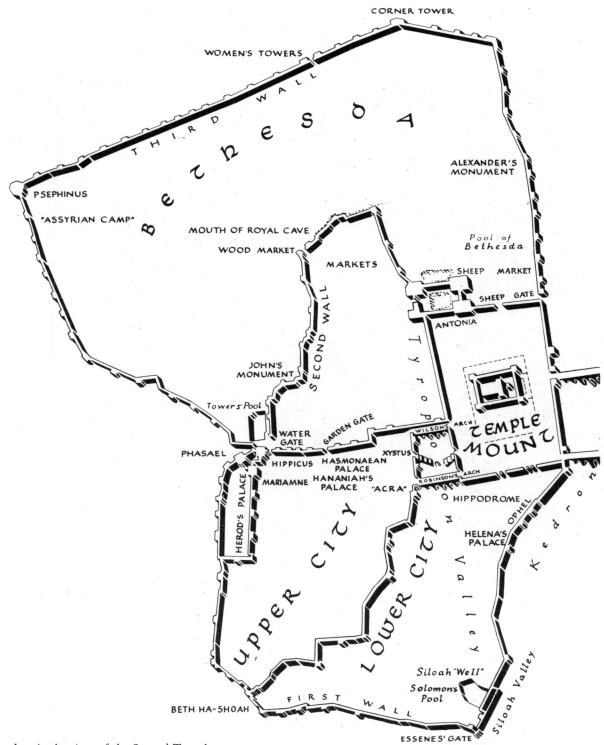

Plan of Jerusalem in the time of the Second Temple.

The "Pool of Hezekiah"—This is
the Amygdalon (Towers') Pool of
the Second Temple period.

General view of the Moslem Quarter of the Old City.

One of the eight sides of the octagon-shaped Dome of the Rock.

The Dome of the Chain, also known as The Tribunal of the Prophet David, on the Temple Mount. Legend has it that in Israelite times, a great chain was suspended from this dome. Litigants or witnesses about to testify had to grasp the chain. When anyone lied, a link would fall from the chain.

Dome of the Chain—Interior.

The Dome of the Rock, principal Moslem sanctuary in Jerusalem and, after the Kaaba at Mecca, and the Mosque at Medina, the third holiest place in Islam. It was built in 691 by the Umayyad Caliph Abd el-Malik.

Detail of mosaic in the Dome of the Rock, containing part of a dedicatory inscription.

Interior of the Dome of the Rock.

This public fountain *(sabil)* was built by the Mameluke Sultan Qait Bey (1468-1496).

Preaching pulpit of *mimbar* near the Dome of the Rock

Recess in the outer wall of the Dome of the Rock paved with Turkish glazed tiles in the 16th century.

The Zion Gate in the Turkish wall
of the Old City near Mt. Zion.

THE WAR OF BAR KOKHBA

Jerusalem was not yet dead, however. The presence of a Roman legion required the continuation of some sort of civil life. The camp needed accomodation for the soldiers' wives and the merchants accompanying the legion. There is evidence that the Jews continued to inhabit some of Jerusalem and to worship on the ruins of the Temple. In any case, they were not expressly prohibited from doing so, even if the city was now considered the property of the victors.

In 130, however, the Emperor Hadrian visited the city and decided to built a Roman city on the ruins of Jewish Jerusalem. The threatened desecration of the city, which would presumably end all hope for its restoration, sparked the War of Bar Kokhba (132-135), also known as the "Second Roman War." After careful planning, the forces of Bar Kokhba overran the Judean plain, cutting off the Roman garrison in Jerusalem from its commander, the Governor of Judea in Caesarea. Shortly afterwards, the legion and the Roman civilians left Jerusalem and the Jews triumphantly occupied it. That some form of Temple worship

Tile stamp of the Tenth Legion Fretensis which camped in the Jerusalem area from the time of Titus till the end of the 3rd century. The ship and boar shown here comprised the Legion's emblem.

was reinstituted we know from the appearance of the image of the Sanctuary on the coins of Bar Kokhba.

In 134, when a ring of Roman armies began to close in, Bar Kokhba evacuated Jerusalem and concentrated his resistance in the Fortress of Beit-Ter, or Bettir, in the mountains several miles to the west. Even after the loss of the city Bar Kokhba struck coins, whose legend, "For the Freedom of Jerusalem," bears eloquent witness to his and his warriors' aims.

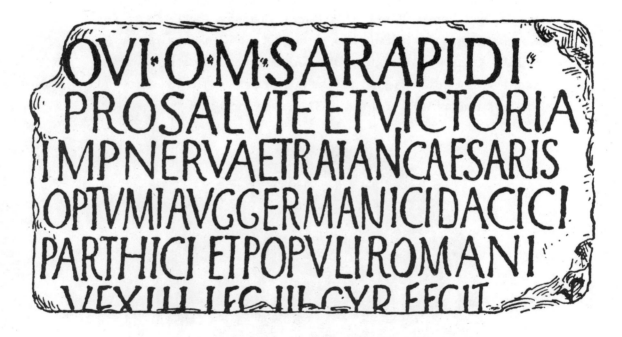

Inscription in Latin to the god Serapis left by
soldiers of the Third Legion, who passed by
Jerusalem in the time of Trajan.

AELIA CAPITOLINA

When Beit-Ter fell a year later, Hadrian proceeded to carry out his plans. The Roman Governor Tineius Rufus had Jewish Jerusalem plowed under and the new city was established as a Roman colony in the shape of a camp. Today the Old City, with its square shape and two roads intersecting each other at right angles, still bears the stamp of the Roman colony. The new Roman city was called *Aelia Capitolina,* in honor of Hadrian, whose full name was Titus Aelius Hadrianus, and the Capitoline Triad, the principal Roman deities. Like all Roman cities, it was equipped with a forum or market adjoining a Temple of Aphrodite, baths, a theater, and a municipal organization based on twelve districts. The temple area, renamed "Quadra" (The Square), was now occupied by a temple of the Capitoline Triad with a statue of Hadrian in front.

Circumcised persons were forbidden to enter the city or even to approach its vicinity beyond a line extending from Beit Horon to Bethel and Beit Zur. This applied also to the Jewish Christian community. Although the community had left Jerusalem during the first siege and had refused to help Bar Kokhba, it was now expelled from the city. Thus, the Christian leadership as well as the traditional information concerning the Christian holy sites now passed to the Christians of non-Jewish extraction.

We have almost no information on Jerusalem as an insignificant Roman provincial city. The legion was stationed there till the end of the third century and we know from inscriptions that the soldiers worshipped various oriental gods, such as the Egyptian Serapis (see illustration). It was in this period that Christian pilgrims began to come to the city. As a matter of fact, in the growing anarchy of the Roman Empire in the third century, Hadrian's edicts fell into disuse and Jewish pilgrims began to visit the Holy City in increasing numbers. Thus we see that Jerusalem was never far from the thoughts and aspirations of the dispersed nation.

THE BYZANTINE PERIOD (324-636)

When Constantine I established Christianity as the official religion of the Roman Empire, the status of Jerusalem was revolutionized. As the site of the last earthly appearance of Jesus, it became the heart of Empire and Church. After Constantine defeated his rival Licinius and extended his sovereignty over the East, his mother, Helena, visited the city. Following this event, Constantine built three churches in the Holy Land—two of them in Jerusalem: the Church of the Resurrection (Anastasis) and the Church of the Eleona on the Mount of Olives. Pilgrimages were encouraged and there was a spate of construction of monasteries and pilgrim hospices. At the same time, Hadrian's ban on the presence of Jews in Jerusalem was again enforced; only on the Fast of the Ninth of Av, the traditional anniversary of the destruction of both Temples, were they allowed to enter and mourn. And when Helena by "divine inspiration" discovered the True Cross in what became the crypt of the Church of the Holy Sepulchre, she set off a chain of events which remolded the image of Jerusalem.

The Emperor Julian "the Apostate" (361-363) thought to arrest this development by restoring Jerusalem as a Jewish city and rebuilding the Temple, but he never managed to implement his plan.

In the centuries that followed Jerusalem prospered. Public and private funds poured into the city, which was now filled with churches and monasteries. Refugees and pilgrims came from all parts of the world. One of the city's outstanding benefactors in this period was the Empress Eudocia, the estranged wife of the Emperor Theodosius II. Among her other works was the extension of the city walls to include "Mount Zion" and the "Ophel" south of the Roman wall. It was due to Eudocia's intervention that Jews were permitted once more to live in Jerusalem.

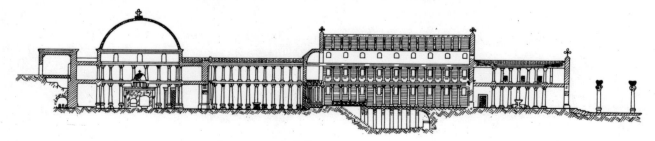

Plan and a section of the Church of the Holy Sepulchre as it was built by the Emperor Constantine on Golgotha (Calvary) Hill.

In the fifth century, Jerusalem was rent by dogmatic disputes which affected it perhaps more than any other city in Christendom. After the Council of Chalcedon in 451, a minor civil war broke out between the various Christian sects.

Early in the sixth century, the Samaritans revolted against Byzantine oppression and ravaged the vicinity of the city. After suppressing the revolt, the Emperor Justinian I (527-565) launched the last glorious period of Byzantine Jerusalem, building the Church of the Virgin Mary and repairing many existing churches.

In the mosaic map discovered in the town of Medeba in Trans-Jordan (see illustration) we have an image of Jerusalem in Justinian's time. We see the city bisected by a colonnaded main street with side streets radiating from it. Its walled interior was filled with churches and monasteries, baths and hospices. Two of Herod's Three Towers still stood at the Jaffa Gate and a column adorned the square inside the Damascus Gate, which the Arabs still call *Bab el-Amud*—"Gate of the Column".

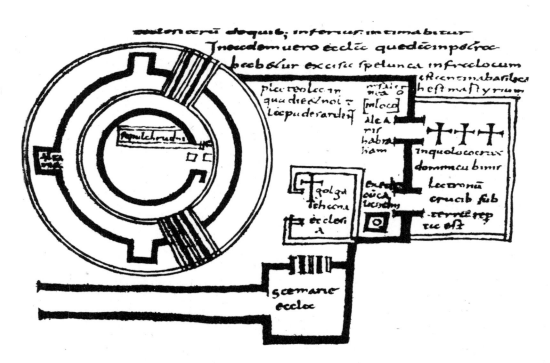

Plan of the Church of the Holy Sepulchre as it was rebuilt after the Persian destruction in 614.

THE PERSIAN AND ARAB CONQUESTS
(614-1099)

After Justinian, Byzantine Jerusalem began to decay. The stream of capital which had spurred the city's economic development dried up, causing prices to skyrocket and wages to plummet. Discontent grew. The loss of popular support was clear when Byzantine rule was put to the test by the Persian invasion in 614. When the invaders, supported by Jewish troops, appeared before the city, the Patriarch Zacharias advised surrender. Others favored resistance. Finally the city was taken by storm and most of its churches, including the Church of the Holy Sepulchre, perished in flames. They were rebuilt by Modestus, who succeeded Zacharias when the latter died in exile.

Byzantine rule was restored for a short time by the Emperor Heraclius in 622. He brought the True Cross back from Persian captivity and again banished the Jews from the city. Soon, however, his armies were sent reeling by the Arab Moslem invaders. In 638 Jerusalem was besieged by the Moslems for four months until the Patriarch Sophronius arranged for its surrender to the Caliph Omar in person.

Following the Arab conquest, the Jews were re-admitted to Jerusalem. Soon after, the *Gaonim*, who constituted the supreme Jewish religious authority in the Holy Land, moved their seat from Tiberias to Jerusalem, where it remained till the 11th century.

Jerusalem enjoyed peace during the reign of the three Orthodox Caliphs and their successors, the Umayyad dynasty. Now the Arabs located their provincial capital at Ramleh, near Jaffa, and Jerusalem did not again become the center of this area until the 19th century. From a religious point of view, however, the Moslems accounted Jerusalem as second in holiness only to Mecca and Medina. To assert this claim, Caliph Abd el-Malik in

Early Arab coin minted in Jerusalem.

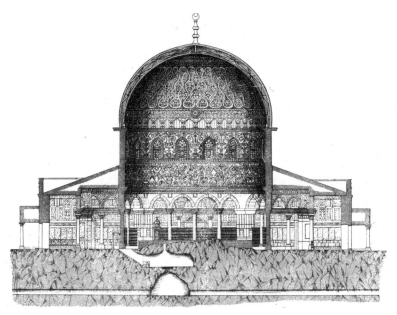

Section of the Dome of the Rock.

691 built the magnificent Dome of the Rock on the Temple Mount. Popularly called the Mosque of Omar because of the legend that he selected the place as the site of a Moslem sanctuary when he took the city in 638, it is called the Dome of the Rock because of the large rock in the center of its floor. According to Jewish tradition it is the rock on which Abraham was prepared to sacrifice his son Isaac; according to Moslem tradition it was Ishmael, the founder of the Arab race, who was to be sacrificed here, and from here Mohammed rode into Heaven on his favorite steed, Baraq. It is also believed to be the site of the threshing floor which David bought from the Jebusite Ornan or Araunah. Scholars declare this to be the site of the Temple's Holy of Holies or the Great Altar (see illustrations). When the Abbasid dynasty acceded to the throne, they transferred the capital of the Arab empire to Baghdad in 763. Conditions in Palestine now took a turn for the worse, with Jerusalem the first to suffer. By the ninth century the Abbasid dynasty had decayed and the real power passed to Turkish mercenaries, the Seljuks. These oppressed the Christian pilgrims who still came to Jerusalem, exacting heavy tolls from them and generally harassing them. The fear and hatred they inspired in Christian Europe remained even after the Egyptian Fatimid dynasty wrested Jerusalem from Abbasid control in the 10th century. And the Fatimid Caliph Hakim indicated his position when he ordered the destruction of the Church of the Holy Sepulchre, a decree which was partly carried out.

The fear for the safety of the holy places was one of the chief factors that led to the Crusades.

Early Arabic inscription concerning the rights of admittance to the Church of the Holy Sepulchre. The custodianship of the Church is hereditary in a Jerusalem Moslem family which keeps the keys.

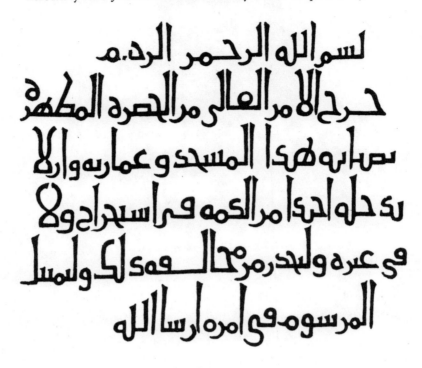

THE CRUSADER KINGDOM OF JERUSALEM
1099-1187

Towards the end of the 11th century there began in Europe the great movement of European chivalry—particularly that of France, Burgundy and Normandy—for the redemption of the Tomb of Christ from the Infidels. The First Crusade, led by Godfrey of Bouillon, reached the walls of Jerusalem after a march of several years across Asia Minor and Syria. On July 15, 1099 the Crusaders stormed the city. In the carnage that followed, the Moslem population was exterminated and the Jews burnt in their synagogue. The conquering knights divided the city's houses and palaces among themselves. Godfrey assumed the title "Protector of the Holy Sepulchre" and his successor, Baldwin I, named himself King of Jerusalem.

Under Crusader rule, Jerusalem was largely a European city. The king lived in the Mosque el-Aqsa till a royal palace was built on the site of Herod's Citadel. The Dome of the Rock became the seat of the Templar

A 19th-century etching of the Citadel of Jerusalem, as it appeared in Turkish times.

The east gate of the Old City, known as St. Stephen's Gate—after the proto-martyr of the Christian Church—and "Lady Mary's Gate," because it leads to the Tomb of the Virgin. Nearby stands the Church of St. Anne.

General view of the eastern section of the Old City, including the Temple Mount. In the background is the Mount of Olives with its churches.

Old City street at night. The public fountain *(sabil)* at left is one of many built by the Turkish Sultan Suleiman I (the Magnificent) in the 16th century.

17th-century Turkish house, one of
the few houses of the period which
stood outside the Old City wall.

The Christian Quarter of the Old City. In the background are (left) the two citadel towers, that on the left built on the base of the Herod's Tower of Phasael.

General view of the Monastery of the Cross (see p. 94). This structure built by Georgian Kings in the 12th century, was built like a fortress to protect the Monastery against attacking robber bands. It is located in a valley in the New City which then was far from town.

The Italian Hospital in the New City, built in the 19th century in the Florentine style.

Road along the Old City wall leading to the Wailing Wall.

A rabbi's signature (18th century).

Interior of the Yohanan Ben Zakkai Synagogue in the Old City, named for the 1st-century Jewish sage. The synagogue was destroyed during the Israel-Arab War.

Street in the Meah Shearim Quarter of the New City. Founded in 1877 by Orthodox European Jews from the Old City, this was one of the first quarters to be built outside the wall.

Jews buying *lulavim* (palm fronds) for the rites of the Feast of Tabernacles in the Meah Shearim market.

Sukkah booths in a courtyard of the Hungarian Houses near Meah Shearim.

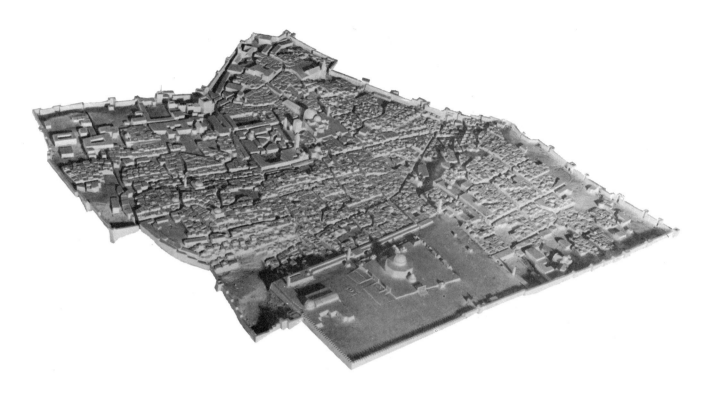

The Old City from the east—a model.

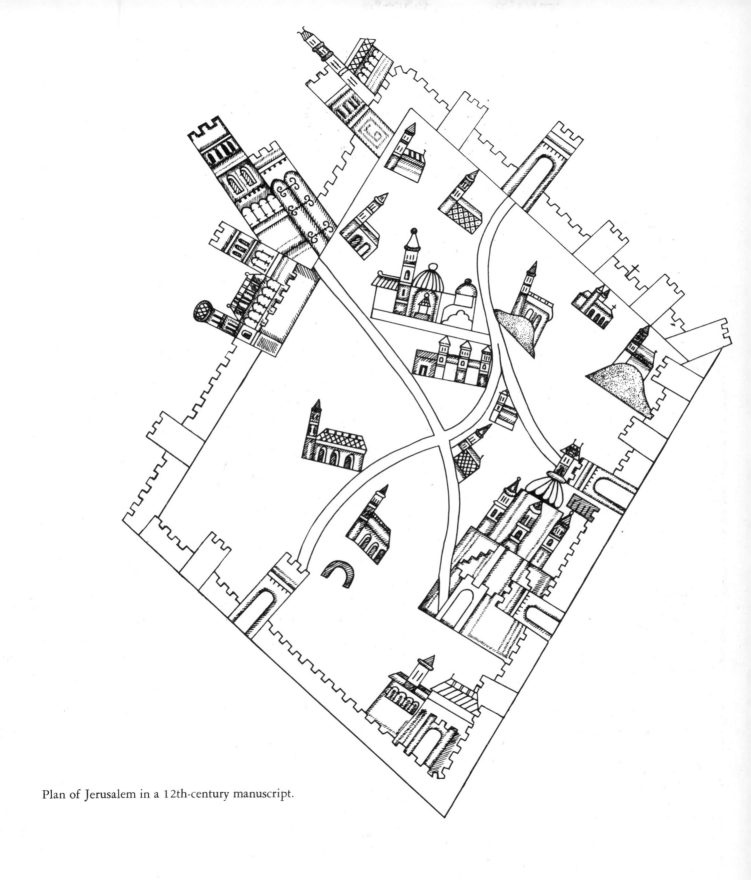

Plan of Jerusalem in a 12th-century manuscript.

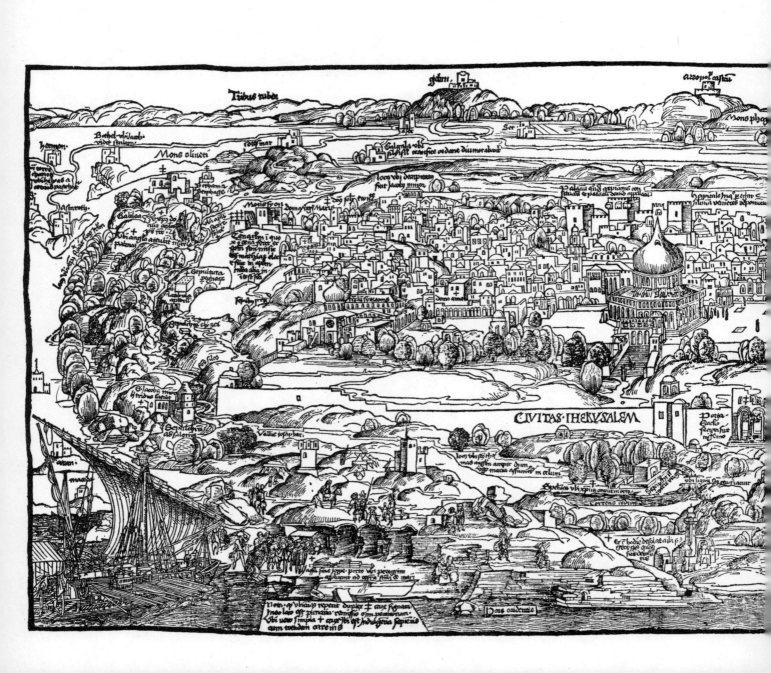

A Crusader knight.

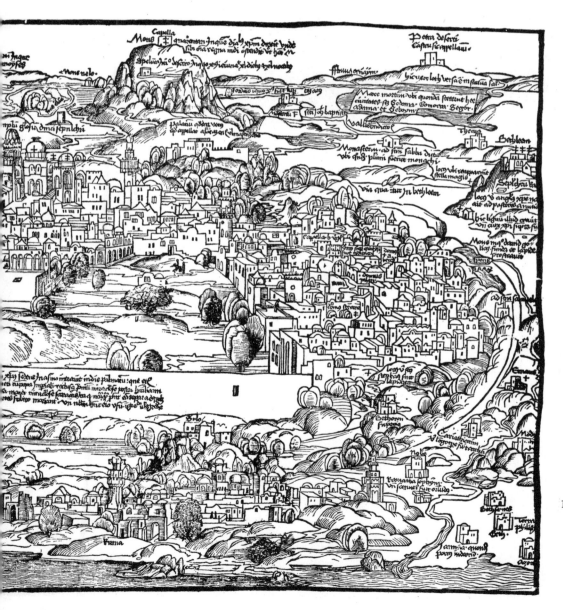

14th-century woodcut of Jerusalem.

Facade of the Mosque el-Aqsa. The mosque stands on substructures dating from the time of the First Temple.

Order, who believed this mosque to represent the Temple of Solomon and organized themselves to be the "Guardians of the Temple." Because of this belief, Templar churches all over Europe were patterned after the mosque. Another great order founded in Jerusalem was the Knights Hospitaler of St. John of Jerusalem. They built their headquarters near the Church of the Holy Sepulchre, which was rebuilt in the form it has today. A third order which figures in this period was the Teutonic Order, organized in 1191 for service in the Holy Land.

Crusader Jerusalem was enclosed within the Roman wall. It had four gates: St. Stephen's Gate on the north, David's Gate on the west, Zion Gate on the south and the Gate of Jehoshaphat on the east. The city abounded with markets and small industries which supplied the needs of the populace and the pilgrims. The pilgrim throngs made necessary a money changers' bazaar, operated mainly by "Syrians," that is Christians

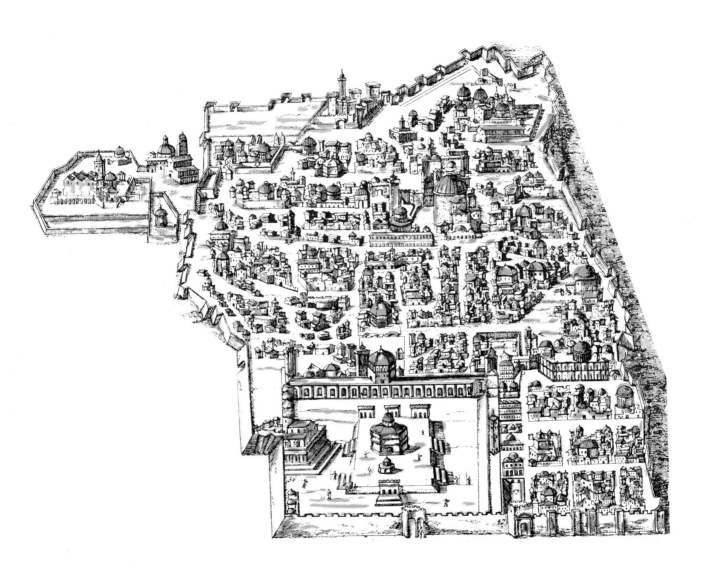

17th-century etching of Jerusalem.

Greek Orthodox monk in the Old City.

Russian pilgrims to Jerusalem in the 19th century.

Slopes of the Mount of Olives, showing the Catholic and Russian Orthodox Churches of Gethsemane.

Traditional site of the Praetorium—the Judgment Hall of the Romans—where the Via Dolorosa begins, as it appeared in the 16th century.

Coin of Baldwin I, the Latin King of Jerusalem from 1100 to 1118. The reverse shows the Citadel of Jerusalem ("Tower of David"), which was the palace of the Crusader monarchs in the center, the Dome of the Rock (right) and (left) the Church of the Holy Sepulchre.

Seal of the Templar Order which was established by the Crusaders in Jerusalem in 1118 to protect pilgrims and the Holy Sepulchre. On the obverse is the Dome of the Rock, which the Crusaders believed to be Solomon's Temple, and the reverse shows two poor knights riding one horse.

of oriental origin. The "Syrians" inhabited the present Moslem Quarter together with the Jews who over the years had been gradually re-admitted to Jerusalem. The Jews engaged mainly in the dyeing trade.

In 1187, the city capitulated to Saladin after he routed the Crusader army at Karnei Hittin in the Galilee. The Moslem sanctuaries were restored and remained in Moslem hands even during the brief renewal of Christian rule under Frederic II (1229-1244). All other Christian attempts to retake the Holy City failed. The Crusader Kingdom maintained itself on the Mediterranean coast till 1291, with its capital at Acre. With the occupation of Jerusalem by Khwarezmian Turks in 1244, Christian rule in Jerusalem ceased till the British occupation in 1917.

Crusader knights storm a city.

Entrance to the Tomb of the Virgin Mary in the Valley of Jehoshaphat. The facade was built in the time of the Crusades.

MAMELUKE AND TURKISH RULE (1244-1799)

The Aiyubids, the successors of Saladin, were soon superseded by their slave guards, the so-called Mamelukes. The Mameluke sultans were the lords of the Holy City from the fourteenth to the sixteenth century. At the beginning they were afraid of another attempt by the Crusaders and dismantled the walls of the city, but these were soon rebuilt. Although Mameluke rule was by its nature unstable, this did not affect Jerusalem overmuch, as politics played no role in the life of the city proper. On the other hand, between 1305 and 1440, the art-loving sultans enriched the Holy City with 39 Moslem schools, monasteries, mosques and other buildings. The Mamelukes allowed the renewal of Christian pilgrimages

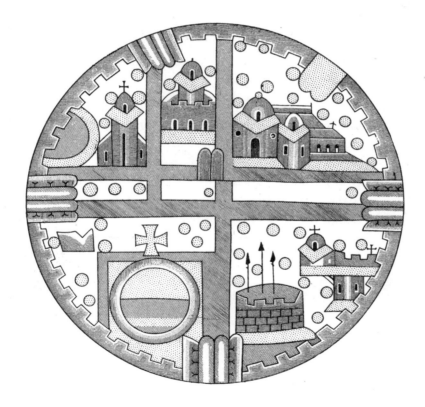

Crusader map of the Holy Land with Jerusalem in the center.

to Jerusalem from which they derived great profit. The Jews also returned as a community in 1190 and were strengthened by successive groups of immigrants in 1211 and 1267. At the end of the Mameluke period the community comprised 150-250 families.

In 1516 the Ottoman Sultan Selim I defeated the Mamelukes and occupied Jerusalem. At first Turkish rule was energetic. Selim's son, Suleiman (the Magnificent) I, gave the city walls their present shape and built many public fountains *(sabils)*. Soon, however, the unruly soldiers and the corrupt pashas gained the upper hand and the population sank to a new low ten thousand, about one third of which were Christians and a tenth Jews.

Turkish infantryman and cavalryman.

Turkish governors and officers had batons carried before them decorated with as many horsetails as their rank entitled them to.

Water vendors in the Old City
carrying their wares in waterskins.

Kebab vendor in the Old City.

Vaulted bazaar in the Old City.

16th-century mosque in the New City which contains the tomb of Nebi Uqashi, one of Mohammed's companions. Adjoining the mosque are the imposing headquarters of the Jerusalem Workers' Council.

Moslem graves in Mamillah Cemetery in the New City.

An Arab public scribe in the Old City writes letters and other documents for those who themselves never learned to write.

Lane in the Moslem Quarter of the Old City at night.

19th-century etching showing man fluffing cotton.

The Abyssinian Church in the New City, built in 1886.

The Russian Cathedral in the New City, occupying the highest ground in the Russian Compound. On this ground Sennacherib and his Assyrian legions camped when they besieged Jerusalem in 701 B.C. (see p. 138). Here again in A.D. 70 the Roman legions of Titus closed ranks before mounting the assault on the Second Temple.

An Abyssinian priest praying.

Detail of a Mosaic in the
Monastery of the Cross.

Corridor in the Catholic Church of Gethsemane.

Entrance to Yemin Moshe, one of
the first Jewish quarters outside the
Old City walls.

Rehov Haneviim (Propnets' Street) in the New City, showing typical architecture of the end of the Turkish period.

Beit Israel Quarter in the New City.

A courtyard in the old section of New Jerusalem.

The windmill built by Sir Moses Montefiore in the Yemin Moshe quarter, one of the first to be built outside the Old City walls in the middle of the 19th century.

The Hebrew University buildings on Mount Scopus. This area, though cut off from Israel, is in Israeli hands.

The United Nations Headquarters building, in the demilitarized zone, which was formerly the residence of the British Mandatory High Commissioner for Palestine.

The mouth of Hezekiah's Tunnel, which still carries the waters of the Gihon to the Pool of Siloam. The Jordanian Arab villagers of Siloam use the waters for washing and irrigation.

The opening ceremony of the Hebrew University in 1925.

The Y.M.C.A. building in the New City, whose Jesus Tower is the highest structure in the New City.

The "Jewish Agency Building," which was the center of world Jewish life till the State of Israel was established. Left is the Palestine Foundation Fund (Keren Hayessod), center—the Jewish Agency proper; right—the Jewish National Fund (Keren Kayemet).

The Bezalel National Museum, founded in 1906, was built in the form of an ancient city wall.

The American Consulate, one of the first buildings of the New City, was built in traditional style.

Lane in Meah Shearim.

The lively street bazaar in the Orthodox Meah Shearim quarter preceding the Feast of Tabernacles (*Sukkot*).

JEWS IN MAMELUKE JERUSALEM

Under the Mamelukes, the Jews gradually rebuilt their community life after the ravages of the Crusader period. At first, the community consisted almost entirely of Jews of the Sefardi rite—that is, those of Spanish and Portugese origin who had immigrated there voluntarily. This element was considerably augmented by the Jews who came to the Holy Land after the

A rabbi's signature (18th cent.).

Spanish expulsion of 1492. Over the following two centuries, considerable numbers of Jews came, individually or in groups, from Germany and Eastern Europe. These were the Jews of the Ashkenazi rite, and soon Jerusalem's Jewish community life was organized into two groups, the Sefardi—which included the Oriental communities—and the Ashkenazi, each with its own synagogues, charity institutions, rabbis, etc. The Chief Rabbi of Jerusalem, however, was usually a Sefardi, and the community enjoyed religious autonomy.

The community supported itself mainly from the crafts. In the source books of the period, we read mainly of dyeing, the clothing industry, shoemaking, weaving—especially of silk. Some engaged in the spice trade or were itinerant peddlers in the settlements around Jerusalem. There were also many rabbis and professional scholars, whose lot was, however, difficult.

Throughout the Mameluke period, the synagogues were often seized and destroyed by the authorities.

In the Ottoman Turkish period that followed, the community suffered from the exactions of the Pashas—the regional governors or tax collectors.

Throughout the Mameluke and Turkish period, the Jews of Jerusalem were in regular contact with the Jews of the Diaspora, through the special emissaries they sent abroad to raise money for their institutions, scholars and needy. We even read of Palestinian emissaries who reached North and South America.

Although material difficulties and governmental oppression prevented Jewish community life from prospering in the City during this period, its existence was never seriously threatened because of the attraction the city held for Jews everywhere.

A decisive change for the better came with the increase of European influence in the 19th century.

Signatures of the members of a Jerusalem *Beit Din* (Rabbinical Court) in the 15th century.

THE LAST CENTURY OF TURKISH RULE

In the eighteenth century, the Holy City knew a period of relative calm. This was a time marked by the gradual strengthening of the Jewish community by various Jewish Hassidic groups who came from Eastern Europe. In 1799, there occurred an event which did not affect Jerusalem directly, but which had far-reaching consequences for its future. In that year, the French Army led by Napoleon invaded Palestine. Although eventually defeated before the walls of Acre and forced to retreat, this first European intrusion into the Holy Land since the Crusades proved decisively that the Orient was no longer capable of defending itself. It took the intervention of another European power, the British fleet, to compel Napoleon to draw back. Following this lesson, unforgettable to all Orientals, came the re-organization of Egypt along European lines and the invasion of Syria by Ibrahim Pasha on behalf of his father Mohammed Ali, the ruler of the

Nile Valley. Jerusalem was occupied in 1831 and remained for ten years under Egyptian rule, which could not be shaken by the revolt of the Palestine Arab peasants. The peasants, exasperated by the new double evils of conscription and taxation, actually occupied Jerusalem, but they were soon dislodged. It took the intervention of the European powers hostile to Mohammed Ali to force the Egyptians out and even then the Turks who returned were not the same as those who had been forced out. They, too, had learned the elements of efficient administration, and henceforward Jerusalem was governed with a much stronger hand, aided by the telegraph and improved roads. In order to keep the various Christian sects under control—now doubly dangerous to the Turkish rulers because each was "protected" by a European power, the Greek Orthodox by the Russians, the Catholics by the French and Austrians and the Protestants by the British and Prussians—and in order to maintain the status quo concerning the guardianship of the holy places, the Turkish government made Jerusalem and the whole of Southern Palestine a separate district, directly dependent upon Constantinople.

Now Western ideas and techniques began to sweep the Holy Land, brought by the Europeans who came in increasing numbers to visit or settle in Jerusalem. The European "invasion" was backed by the powerful foreign consulates, each under the protection of its capitulary rights, which practically exempted foreigners from Turkish jurisdiction. Each consulate had its own guard, its own courts, its own post office, etc. To accomodate the thousands of Russian pilgrims who streamed annually into the Holy City, the Russian Mission built a whole compound of hospices and hospitals around a typically Russian cathedral. The Germans built the "German Colony," a garden city of their own in the Valley of Rephaim; then after the state visit of Kaiser Wilhelm II the Abbey of the Dormition on Mt. Zion and the Victoria-Augusta Hospice on Mt. Scopus were constructed. The French built the first railway to Jerusalem in the eighties, and were ably represented by a series of scientific bodies. It was with the first visit of the American Bible scholar, Dr. E. Robinson, after whom "Robinson's Arch" is named (see illustration), that the archeological study of Jeru-

salem took a scientific turn. In the sixties and seventies began the long series of American, British and French excavations which have furnished us with most of our knowledge of ancient Jerusalem. In the sixties, too, the first exact plan of the city was efficiently produced by the British Ordance Survey.

The Jews of Jerusalem had sought at an early date to secure the protection of the European consulates, in particular those of Britain and Germany. From a mere handful of 1,500 souls in 1827, they increased by 1873 to 10,600, thus becoming a majority in the city for the first time since 70 A.D. By 1910 they constituted 50,000 of the 68,000 inhabitants. In the middle of the 19th century, they began to live beyond the confines of the Old City. The first quarter built outside the walls was Mazkeret Moshe, initiated and financed by Sir Moses Montefiore and Judah Touro (see illustrations). This was followed by Yemin Moshe, then by the populous Meah Shearim and Beit Israel quarters in the seventies. In the next decades the Mahane Yehudah Quarter and its dependencies were built along the Jaffa Road, extending the city beyond the watershed line for the first time in history. At the same time the Bukharian Quarter brought the city to the Upper Kidron Valley and finally, just before World War I, the Zikhron Moshe quarter was built along more modern European lines.

During all this time most of Jewish Jerusalem lived in the traditional way. The year smoothly went its way from festival to festival—from the High Holy Days to the Feast of Tabernacles, followed by Hanukah and Purim, Passover and Shavuot, interspersed with the days of mourning and fasting and the weekly Sabbath. The population largely comprised the Talmudic scholars and their families who were dependent on support from abroad. But even their strongly entrenched mode of life began to give way: schools approaching a European standard were opened, arts and crafts were taught at the Bezalel Art School, public libraries were introduced and small industry, mostly printing and the production of religious articles, began to develop. By 1907, modernism had made such headway in Jerusalem that there occurred the first workers' strike in the city—characteristically in the printing trade—led by the young Zionist labor leader, today the President of Israel, Mr. Izhak Ben-Zvi.

WORLD WAR I AND THE BRITISH MANDATE

The First World War, in which Turkey and Britain confronted each other across the Suez Canal, was a period of much suffering in Jerusalem, and famine and plague reduced the population to below 50,000. Finally, the bloodless capture of the city by the British forces under General Allenby on December 9, 1917 restored the city to Christian rule, after four hundred years of Turkish and nearly 1,300 years of only occasionally-interrupted Moslem dominion.

The Balfour Declaration, issued by the British Government five weeks before the capture of Jerusalem, raised high hopes for the re-establishment of a Jewish national home in the Holy Land. When the war ended and the British Mandate in Palestine was confirmed, the increasing Jewish immigration began to be felt in the capital no less than in the outlying areas.

Windmill in Yemin Moshe built by Sir Moses Montefiore.

For a great part of Jerusalem, the new British administration was the only sign of the changing times. In the Moslem quarters and the areas dominated by the Christian churches, the even tenor of life continued with all the color of oriental life. The changes noted here concerned mainly international politics: with the fall of Czarist Russia the Orthodox Church lost its mainstay, the Armenian, Coptic and Abyssinian churches increased their foothold, and the Roman Catholics held their own.

Dancing in the streets on Simhat Torah—Feast of the Rejoicing of the Law. In the background is Hechal Shlomo, seat of the Chief Rabbinate.

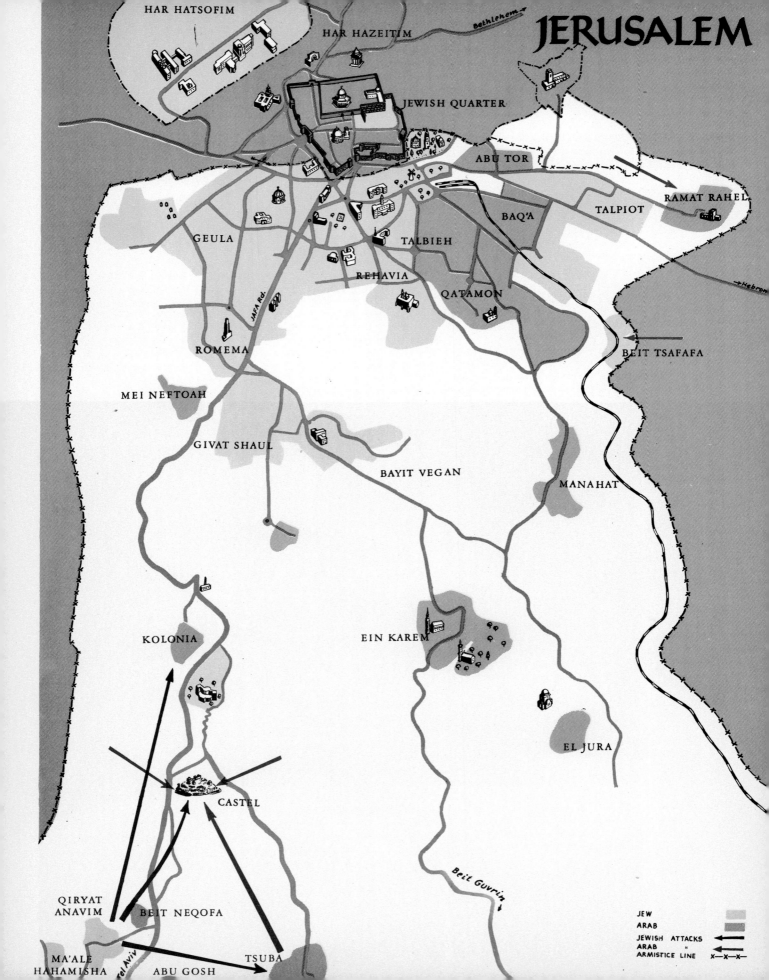

JERUSALEM

HAR HATSOFIM

HAR HAZEITIM

Bethlehem

JEWISH QUARTER

ABU TOR

RAMAT RAHEL

TALPIOT

BAQ'A

GEULA

TALBIEH

Hebron

REHAVIA

QATAMON

ROMEMA

BEIT TSAFAFA

MEI NEFTOAH

GIVAT SHAUL

BAYIT VEGAN

MANAHAT

KOLONIA

EIN KAREM

EL JURA

CASTEL

Beit Guvrin

QIRYAT
ANAVIM

BEIT NEQOFA

TSUBA

MA'ALE
HAHAMISHA

Tel Aviv

ABU GOSH

JEW

ARAB

JEWISH ATTACKS

ARAB "

ARMISTICE LINE   x—x—x

Battle map of the War of Liberation.

The shelling of Jerusalem by enemy artillery during the 1948 siege.

Ben-Yehuda Street, one of the New City's main streets, as it appeared right after an explosion which shattered it at the beginning of the War of Liberation.

Scout in the Jerusalem hills during the War of Liberation.

Supply convoys to besieged Jerusalem were attacked on the way to the city from the Coastal Plain. Strewn along the sides of the road are the shells of wrecked vehicles.

Armored car stuck amid the ruins.

Defenders of Jewish Jerusalem.

Supply convoy arrives from the coast after the siege is lifted.
Center: Precious water was rationed in the besieged city.

Boys plant trees in the hills around the city

New buildi
going up.

It was naturally in the Jewish sector that the greatest changes were wrought. The Jewish population of Jerusalem doubled in the Mandatory period, so that in 1946 they numbered 102,000 out of 165,000. Their economic base was revolutionized. While the main occupations were still metal working, clothing and textiles, carpentry, printing and food handling, the percentage of those engaged in these industries rose. Another significant sign was the increase of those employed in public offices and the professions. With the establishment in Jerusalem of the Mandatory Central Government and the headquarters of the world Zionist bodies, public service became an increasingly important factor in the life of the city. An historic spiritual event was the establishment in 1925 of the Hebrew University on Mount Scopus, which added a new element of scholars and students to the Holy City. This was followed by the New Medical Center and the nucleus of a National Library, also on Mount Scopus. Private building kept pace with public construction, and new Jewish quarters—Rehaviah, Beit Hakerem, Geula and others—covered the gaps between the existing ones and pushed the city westward. In comparison with this dynamic expansion, non-Jewish architectural enterprise was modest: the Government erected a new Post Office and a residence for the High Commissioner; private donations from America financed the construction of the Palestine Archaeological Museum and the new Y.M.C.A.

The expansion of the city in Mandatory times was not as peaceful as had been hoped. The increase of Jewish immigration and the political hopes it aroused led to a hardening of the Arab attitude. Three times, in 1922, 1929 and throughout 1936-1939, the streets of Jerusalem were the scenes of bloody riots instigated by the Arab political and religious leaders. The last period of disturbances, launched with a six-month general strike, led to a division of the city into a Jewish and an Arab Sector, a forerunner of things to come.

WORLD WAR II AND THE STRUGGLE AGAINST MANDATORY RULE (1939-1947)

Paradoxically enough, the years of World War II were comparatively quiet. During this time Jerusalem served as a place of refuge for various persecuted peoples. In 1936, Haile Selassie, Emperor of Abyssinia, came here after he was driven from his homeland by the Italians. He was followed by Poles, Yugoslavs, Greeks and many others.

Yet there was one nation excluded from this haven of refuge. Bowing to Arab violence, the British government of Neville Chamberlain in 1939 published a White Paper, aimed at practically ending Jewish immigration into Palestine. As long as the struggle against Nazi Germany lasted, the Jews volunteered in ever-increasing numbers for the British Army, postponing the all-out struggle against the White Paper. When the war ended, new hopes were raised by the accession of the Labor Government in 1945. When these hopes were disappointed, the struggle broke out with fury. The majority of the Jews fought the Government peacefully, by "illegal" immigration and non-cooperation. But there was a minority which ceaselessly attacked the strongholds of the British regime. Some of the scars of these conflicts are still visible in Jerusalem. The harassed government retaliated with a system of security zones, which turned Jerusalem into a patchwork of barbed-wire compounds from which the police and troops issued to deal with the civilians. Finally, unable to establish order, the Mandatory Government appealed to the United Nations. On November 29, 1947, the United Nations voted to partition Palestine into sovereign Jewish and Arab states.

THE WAR OF LIBERATION AND THE
ISRAEL-ARAB WAR (1947-48)

The U.N. resolution was received with great rejoicing in Jewish Jerusalem; but it launched a period of deadly struggle. On Sunday, November 30, the Arabs ravaged the New City's commercial center and outlying Jewish quarters. Soon the conflict spread. The position of Jewish Jerusalem was very precarious, cut off by forty miles of Arab-held territory from the

ירושלים

Emblem of Jewish Jerusalem. The lion is the symbol of the Tribe of Judah and one of the Biblical names of Jerusalem and the Temple is Ariel—the Lion of God (Isaiah 29:1-2).

compact Jewish settlements in the Coastal Plain. The outpost settlements of Atarot in the north and the Etzion Bloc in the south succumbed to the Arab Legion of Trans-Jordan, the latter after a long resistance against tremendous odds, which gave Jerusalem some breathing time. The cutting of the road to the coast threatened its supplies and the destruction of the water pipeline from *Ras el-Ain* (Rosh Ha'ayin) made the cisterns in the city its only source of water. But it was decided to hold out at all costs. In the beginning of the struggle, many dozens of Jews were killed in explosions set off by British deserters in the center of the New City—on Ben Yehuda Street (see illustration), at the Keren Hayesod building and at the *Jerusalem Post*. The Jewish Quarter in the Old City and the Hebrew University and the Hadassah Hospital on Mount Scopus were cut off. Attempts to send convoys to the threatened areas resulted in heavy losses, and Jewish efforts to take the intervening quarter of Sheikh Jerrah were repulsed by the British. Yet, despite the crippling handicaps placed in their path by the expiring Mandatory Government, the Jews achieved something. A series of big convoys entered the city with precious food and supplies. Just before Passover 1948 the road to the coast was cleared for great stretches and strong points established along it. The capture of the Talbieh and Katamon quarters established a secure link with Talpiyot and Ramat Rahel in the south and barred the road to aggressors from that direction.

With the end of the Mandate and the proclamation of the State of Israel on May 15, 1948, the Jews and Arabs stood face to face. At first, it was the Jews who took the offensive; the road to the Old City was opened and the "security" zones in the center of the New City—popularly known as "Bevingrad," after the British Foreign Minister—were occupied. Soon, however, the regular Arab armies intervened; the Arab Legion attacked in the Old City and took the Jewish Quarter after heavy fighting; the Egyptians attacked in Ramat Rahel but were repulsed. The Jews stood their ground when the Legion turned against the New City and the Arab forces gave vent to their fury by a merciless bombardment of Jewish Jerusalem. They began a siege in the hope of starving the Jews into surrender. This hope, too, was disappointed. Circumventing the Arab positions at Latrun, a new road, the so-called "Burma Road," was opened into the plain and much needed supplies of food and ammunition reached the city shortly before the First Armistice in June, 1948. In the subsequent ten days of fighting in July, the Jewish corridor to the west was widened. The final armistice confirmed the division of the city.

New Jerusalem celebrates Independence Day.

Lighting memorial candles at the traditional Tomb of King David on Mt. Zion.

The ascent to Mt. Zion.

After the Torah has been read in Mt. Zion synagogue, the Scroll is rolled up again, dressed and replaced in the Holy Ark.

178

Independence Menorah in the Knesset Garden, presented to the Israel Knesset (Parliament) by the British Parliament. It was executed by the British sculptor Benno Elkan.

Mr. Itzhak Ben-Zvi, the President of Israel and Mrs. Ben-Zvi stand near the entrance to the Executive Mansion on their departure for Burma.

A Yemenite Jew.

Immigrants from Persia in
their colorful costumes.

180

A Jerusalem youth wearing "Palmach" insignia. The Palmach was the commando section of the pre-state underground.

Ultra-modern villa.

General view of New Jerusalem.

Hebrew University Student Hostel.

Kiryat Hayovel—a new immigrant quarter in Jerusalem's south-western hills.

The Central Post Office on Jaffa Road, only a few dozen yards from the border.

Dedication of the new Hebrew University Campus in 1958.

The I. Goldstein Synagogue at the University Campus.

General view of University Campus.

Blowing of the *Shofar* (Ram's Horn) in pilgrimage ceremony on Mt. Zion.

JERUSALEM IN THE STATE OF ISRAEL

Since 1948, Jerusalem has been a city divided. The Old City and the area
north of it are held by Jordan. This territory has a population of 65,000
(35,000 in the Old City proper).

The New City, including Mount Zion, and the Hebrew University—
Hadassah Hospital enclave on Mount Scopus are in the State of Israel. In
1950, the Government and Parliament (Knesset) moved from Tel Aviv
to Jerusalem.

As a result of the siege, the Jewish population of Jerusalem had declined
to 70,000. Today, it has risen to over 150,000. New quarters for immigrants and veteran residents alike have sprung up on the hills and in the
valleys west of the city as far as Ein Kerem and Motza.

Since the Jordan Government—in breach of the Armistice Agreement—
has denied them access to the Wailing Wall, the Jews have made Mount
Zion near the traditional "Tomb of David" their chief holy place. Colorful ceremonies which recall the days of the Second Temple have been
revived there. Modern Jewish religious life has found its expression in
Hechal Shlomo, the seat of the Chief Rabbinate, with all of Israel's religious communities—Jewish, Christian, Moslem and Druse—served by the
Ministry for Religious Affairs nearby. The Government is gradually setting

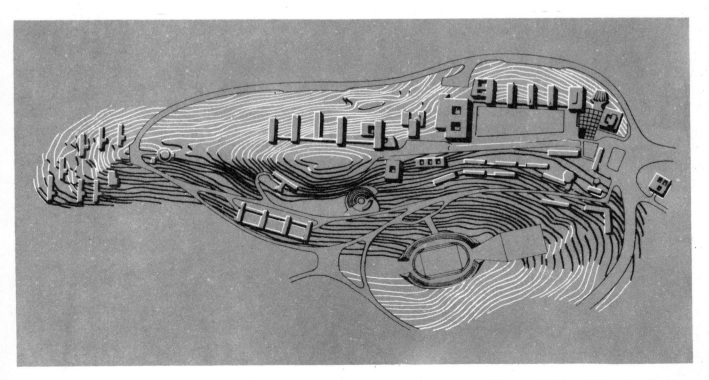

Plan of the new Hebrew University Campus.

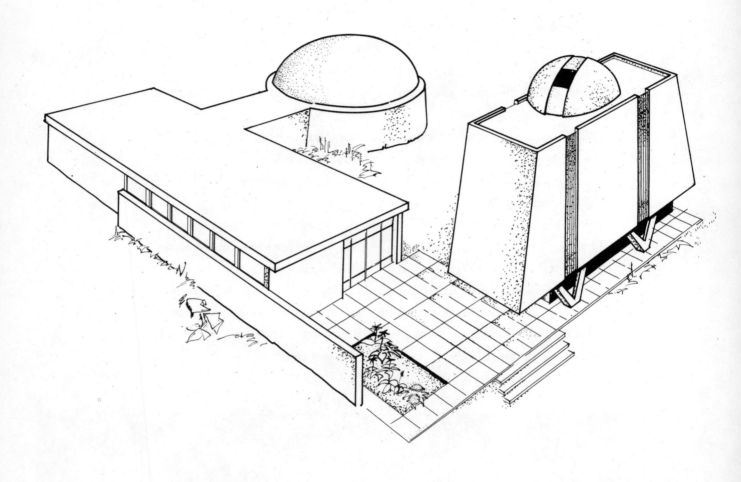

The N.Z. Williams Observatory and Planetarium on the Hebrew University Campus; plan of architect A. Friedman.

up its permanent headquarters in the "Kiryah Hill" west of the city. Adjoining it, the new Hebrew University campus has been built, extending for two miles and already housing most of the schools of the University. Student society is making an increasing mark on the city's life.

While spiritual needs are not being neglected, attention is also being paid to the material side so as to anchor the growing population as far as possible in productive occupations. Industry is being encouraged. According to latest statistics 24 per cent of the populaion is engaged in industry, 15 per cent in trade, 15 per cent in public service, 10 per cent in the professions and 10 per cent in services. The difficulties are admittedly great, as Jerusalem lacks the natural resources for economic development. Yet, the clothing, metals, food and printing industries are making headway. Increased railway facilities, improved roads, the expansion of the water and electrical networks, new parks and schools, all are making New Jerusalem a very pleasant place in which to live

Architect's drawing of the new Hadassah-Hebrew University School of Medicine in the village of Ein Karem, a western suburb of Jerusalem.

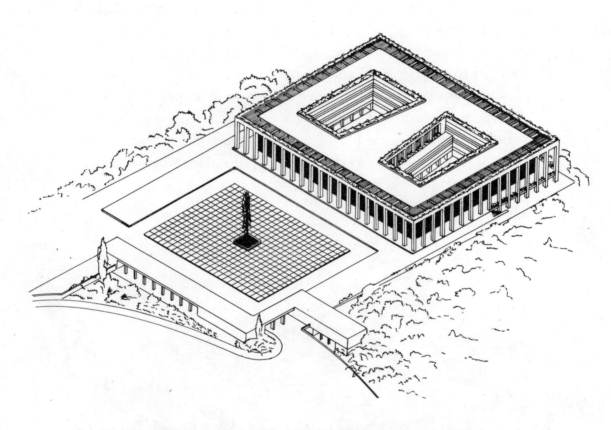

The building to be erected for the Knesset—Israel's Parliament—in Jerusalem; plan of architect J. Klarwein.

CONCLUSION

Jerusalem has in all times been both a symbol and a living city. As a symbol, it has been held sacred by hundreds of millions of people who have never beheld it in reality. It has stood for the noblest human aspirations, which have not been connected to such an extent with any other earthly city. To the Jew in the Diaspora, who devoutly wishes every Passover and Yom Kippur "Next Year in Jerusalem," to the Christian and Moslem, it has symbolized an idea apart from ordinary life, a vision of better things, if not on this earth, then in the celestial regions.

Such high aspirations give Jerusalem its peculiar flavor. But at the same time, it is and always has been a living city. As such it has had its periods of decline, strife, hunger, pestilence, and also its periods of prosperity, material and spiritual. To those living there, it is a city of natural grandeur which even the vilest effors of man could not quite tarnish. It is a city built on hills and in valleys, with sudden views of distant mountains and mysterious seas, with a limpid and serene lucidity in the atmosphere which lends beautiful roseate hues to its stones.

It is still to a large extent removed from the material grossness of our era, and one can only hope that its spiritual influence will again be felt in mankind and that the blessing of old will be implemented: "Peace be within thee" (Ps. 122:7).

Besides editors and assistants whose names appear in Editorial Board list, we were also helped by many scientists, advisors and collectors; therefore, we see it as our duty to express our thanks to all those who lent us a hand in obtaining the pictures or who gave us their advice concerning the material we worked with. Heading the list is His excellency The President of Israel, Mr. I. Ben-Zvi, who not only put at our disposal his library and engravings collection, but was also so kind as to give us his advice in many details involving the gathering and the preparation of the material. We would also like to mention the name of Prof. B. Mazar, President of the Hebrew University, who went over the pictures and text of the book and counselled us as well. In addition, we would like to cite the members of the Archaeology Department of the Hebrew University, headed by Prof. N. Avigad; The Department of Anitquities of the Ministry of Education and Culture; The Bezalel National Museum; The Photography Department of the Jewish Agency; The Keren Hayesod Archives; The Keren Kayemet Le Israel (Jewish National Fund) Photographic Archives; Dr. H. Tadmor; Mr. I. Nadel; Mr. H. Raviv and others. And in foreign countries: The American Geographical Society, New York; The Oriental Instiute of the University of Chicago; Brussels Museum; Yale University, New Haven, Connecticut. We would also like to take this opportunity to thank the Government of Israel and its following departments: The Ministry of Foreign Affairs and Israeli representatives in the U.S.A. and Canada; the Ministry of Education and Culture; the Minstry of Commerce and Industry; the Ministry of the Treasury and the office of the Government Printer, who stood with us and extended their help in every stage since the idea of this project was presented.

We wish to express our deep thanks to Dr. George S. Wise of Mexico; Mr. Allen Bronfman, Mr. Michael Grinblatt, Mr. Joseph Berman, Mr. William Riven and Mr. Joseph Frank of Montreal; Mr. Howard Greenfeld, Mr. Joseph Wunsch and Mr. Daniel Ross of New-York; Mr. Walter Williams and Mr. Jehiel Burla of Jerusalem; Mr. Joshua Ben-Zion of Tel Aviv; and others who helped us throughout our work.

Our thanks also to the management and staff of Schwitter A.G. Lithography, Zurich; Grafor and Omanim Meuchadim, Tel Aviv; E. Pikovsky, Jerusalem; Monson Photolitho Printing Press in Jerusalem and its managing director, Mr. Sh. Monson; Dfus Limmudi at the Brandeis Centre, Jerusalem; Hakorech Binders' Cooperative and Hamerkaz Bindery, Tel Aviv. All these accomplished faithfully the photolitho work, typesetting, composing, printing and binding of this book.

THE PUBLISHERS

PRINTED IN ISRAEL

PRINTING OF COLOR AND BLACK AND WHITE PLATES AND OF THE TEXT AND END PAPER—SH. MONSON,
JERUSALEM. TYPESETTING—THE BRANDEIS CENTER, JERUSALEM. PHOTOLITHO WORK—CLICHÉS SCHWITTER
A. G. ZURICH; GRAFOR, TEL AVIV; UNITED ARTISTS, TEL AVIV; E. PIKOVSKY, JERUSALEM. FOLDING—
HAMERKAZ BINDERS, TEL AVIV. BINDING—HAKORECH BINDERS' COOP., HOLON.
COVER DESIGN—E. PAUKER, JERUSALEM.

"Peace"—Section of the Independence Menorah in the Knesset Garden depicting the prophecy of Isaiah 11:6-8.